THE PREACHER'S CALLING
TO BE SERVANT

The Preacher's Calling to be Servant

by

D. T. NILES

HARPER & BROTHERS

PUBLISHERS · NEW YORK

Except where indicated, Biblical quotations
are from the Revised Standard Version

Library of Congress Catalog Card Number: 59-10349

TO
"THAMBI" SELVARETNAM

Contents

Foreword

WHEN I asked a friend in Scotland who had heard Dr. Niles deliver these Warrack Lectures what he thought about them, his first remark was: "These were not lectures, but sermons." I think he was right and I have reason to believe that my friend D. T. Niles will not quarrel with that description. On the contrary! For while "D.T." (as he is known all over the world) is an ecumenical statesman who presides with remarkable ability over the meetings of the World's Student Christian Federation, who plays an often decisive role in negotiations concerning Church union and who maps out new policies for the Asian Churches and councils in the East Asia Christian Conference, he is and remains first and foremost the pastor, the preacher and the evangelist.

Like his friend and *guru* Pastor Pierre Maury of France, D.T. proves that it is possible to combine the ecumenical with the pastoral tasks, the concern for the whole Church of Christ with the concern for the individual. But he has no doubt that priority must be given to the pastoral. For, as he makes abundantly clear in these pages, the fundamental characteristic of the Christian life is sharing in the ministry of the risen and ascended Lord and this sharing must take the form of direct witness from person to person. A Christian cannot take his stand outside the situation in which his Lord has placed him—the situation of the hearer of the Word, the meaning of whose life is to transmit that Word to his fellow-men. The Christian is never in an

9

impersonal situation in which he can forget the personal God and the persons to whom the Word is to be passed on. So the adequate way to "lecture" about preaching is not to theorize about it but to "preach" about it.

So these pages are really straightforward sermons addressed to "preachers". But by no means only to professional preachers; just as much to Christians who ought to learn again that that good old word "preaching" does not mean talking in a more or less solemn and boring way about religious subjects, but rather the ministry of the living Word of God which transforms human lives. We find it so very difficult in our Western lands to avoid the extremes of a monotonous revivalistic preaching in terms of old clichés on the one hand and learned theological preaching which does not challenge on the other. In that situation Dr. Niles' approach which is at the same time existential and full of the richness of the Biblical message comes as a breath of fresh air.

We can learn in these pages that "the task (of preaching) has a momentum apart from the preacher and that he is carried by it". It happens that I can illustrate this by giving my version of the story about the first meeting between D. T. Niles and myself to which he refers in these pages. For that student conference in Allahabad in 1933 I had prepared an address which showed my interest in certain new theological movements, but revealed also that I knew next to nothing about Indian students. So it seemed quite clear that that address had been a complete failure. It was only years later that I heard from D.T. that this particular address had meant a turning point in his life. The task had shown its momentum apart from the preacher.

W. A. VISSER 'T HOOFT

Introduction

EVERY workman has pride in his work. I am a preacher, and I am proud of the work to which I have committed my life. There is deep satisfaction in making Jesus Christ known and His Gospel understood.

This is the third series of lectures on the work of a preacher which I have been privileged to deliver, and in very real measure the preparation of these series has been also to me a means of grace. They have helped me constantly to remember the nature of the calling by which a preacher is called, and the content of the Gospel which he must proclaim. It is so easy for a preacher to preach, and even to preach well, without being faithful to his message. The voice that bids men prepare the way of the Lord is always and only God's possibility, and the preacher cannot inherit it except by faith.

The preacher's temptation is a besetting one. He is never free from the desire to escape from his original calling and make the determinant of his preaching not the Gospel which alone can save, but the winning of appreciation for his preaching which alone can procure him preference. Where there is faithful preaching it is usually also appreciated, but the problem is that it is possible to win this appreciation without the discipline of being bound by the limitations of the Gospel. This fact—the limitations which the Gospel sets on the preacher because it is the Gospel of Jesus Christ—has been, in a sense, the controlling theme of the three series of lectures to which I have referred.

In 1952 were delivered the Bevan Memorial Lectures at Adelaide in Australia. The title of these lectures was "Preaching the Gospel of the Resurrection". *The message which we preach has been committed to us.* We are called to tell the story of what God has wrought for man in Jesus Christ. "Jesus of Nazareth, a man attested to you by God, you crucified and killed by the hands of lawless men. This Jesus, God raised up, and of that we are all witnesses. Know assuredly, therefore, that God has made him both Lord and Christ. Wherefore repent, and be baptized every one of you in the name of Jesus Christ for the forgiveness of your sins; and you shall receive the gift of the Holy Spirit" (cf. Acts 2: 22–38).

In 1957 were delivered the Lyman-Beecher Lectures at Yale in the United States of America. The title of these lectures was "The Preacher's Task and the Stone of Stumbling". *The reason why we preach is determined for us.* Men must be led into an acceptance of Jesus Christ as the Lord of their lives and as the Saviour of all men. "Behold, I am laying in Zion a stone, a cornerstone chosen and precious, and he who believes in him will not be put to shame. To you therefore who believe, he is precious, but for those who do not believe it has become a stone that will make men stumble, a rock that will make them fall" (cf. 1 Peter 2: 6–8).

Now in 1958, for these Warrack Lectures delivered in Scotland, the title is "The Preacher's Calling to be Servant". *The proof of what we preach is promised to us.* There is no other guarantee of the truth of our witness except that it is caught and held within the witness of the Holy Spirit to Jesus Christ and of Jesus Christ to himself. "It was declared at first by the Lord, and it was attested to us by those who heard him, while God also bore witness by signs and wonders and various miracles and by gifts of the Holy Spirit distributed according to his own will" (Heb. 2: 3–4).

When at Evanston in 1954, at the Second Assembly of the World Council of Churches, I had to deliver one of the evening addresses, I chose as my text the parable of the friend at midnight. That address too I have included in this book as a postscript. It deals with the theme of "the servant-ministry" in terms of our evangelistic calling, and seeks to show how that calling undergirds every Christian vocation.

It is every Christian who shares both in the calling to bear testimony to Jesus Christ and in the calling to partake in the servant-ministry of the Church; but precisely because this is so, it is essential not to obscure the nature and significance of the special calling of "preachers". It is their task not only to bear testimony to Jesus Christ, but also to proclaim "the whole counsel of God" (Acts 20: 27). On their preaching will depend the intelligibility of the testimony of their fellow Christians. Also, it is their task so to partake in the servant-ministry of the Church that they are them-selves established and recognized as "servants through Jesus" (2 Cor. 4: 5, R.V. marginal reading). The layman is normally engaged in some form of service in the secular world; it is the "preacher" who needs to be so established. He needs to find full participation in the lay office of the Church.

I did not find it hard to decide to whom to dedicate this book. I have dedicated it to Selvaretnam, my closest friend from schooldays, who through years of devoted service to others has earned the name of "Thambi"—"younger brother". Among those I have had the privilege to know intimately, he has helped me best to understand the true implication of a preacher's calling to be servant.

> Sovereign Lord, who didst make the heaven and the earth and the sea and everything in them, who didst say by the Holy Spirit,
>
> > the kings of the earth set themselves in array
> > and the peoples imagine vain things against
> > the Lord and against his Anointed,
>
> look now upon their threats, and grant to thy servants to speak thy word with all boldness, while thou stretchest out thy hand to heal, and signs and wonders are performed through the name of thy holy servant Jesus. Amen.
>
> (Cf. Acts 4: 24–31.)

1

It is the Father who remains ever in me, who is
performing his own deeds. Truly, truly, I tell you,
he who believes in me will do the very deeds I do,
and still greater deeds than these. For I am going
to the Father, and I will do whatever you ask in
my name.

I will ask the Father to give you another Helper
to be with you for ever, even the Spirit of truth.

Peace I leave to you, my peace I give to you;
I give it not as the world gives its "Peace!" Let
not your hearts be disquieted or timid.

(John 14: 10, 12, 16, 17, 27, 28, Moffatt.)

Almighty God, give us grace to be not only hearers but
doers of thy holy word, not only to admire but to obey thy
doctrine, not only to profess but to practise thy religion,
not only to love but to live thy gospel. So grant that what
we learn of thy glory we may receive into our hearts and
show forth in our lives, through Jesus Christ our Lord.
Amen.

Prayer for the Lambeth Conference, 1948 (S.P.C.K.).

1. The Calling of a Preacher

*You know the word which he sent to Israel, preaching
good news of peace by Jesus Christ (he is Lord of all).*
(Acts 10: 36.)

In these Warrack Lectures we shall seek to consider
not so much the task of preaching as the calling of a
preacher. A preacher is certainly called to preach, but
the essence of his calling is that it is concerned not
simply with something he must do but primarily with
something he must be. His call is not just a call to
preach, it is the call to be a preacher. It is a person
whom the call defines and not merely a task.

Everyone who has committed himself in discipleship
to Jesus Christ is a person with a call to preach. On him
rests the unavoidable responsibility of giving a reason
for the hope that is in him. (1 Pet. 3: 15.) He has the
obligation to make Jesus known and loved and obeyed.
Also, as Christ's disciple, he has the duty to live as
Christ would have him live in the world, unconformed
to the world's standards (Rom. 12: 2) and yet "salt"
in effective association with the world for the sake of
which the salt exists. (Matt. 5: 13.)

My father was a lawyer and later a judge. A great
part of his working life, therefore, was naturally spent
in the law-courts and the law-library. When he died,
many of his lawyer friends—most of them Hindus—said
to me, "Your father was a minister more than he was
a lawyer. We not only respected him as the leading
civil lawyer in the courts, but more than that we looked

up to him because he was a kind of elder brother to us all. His moral standards were high and he maintained them, and with all of us his personal relationships were kindly. His influence in the law-library was a felt-influence." Just three months ago, I was looking through and sorting out my father's papers, and among them I found a copy of an address he had delivered on "Church policy and the evangelistic life of the Church". In this address occurred the following paragraph:

> Christians must move intimately with non-Christians in all social and political functions which are definitely righteous. A fellowship between Christians and non-Christians must arise, and it must be made easy and natural for non-Christians to respond to Christian invitations to Christian meetings. Educated Hindus who are near to Christianity must be able to find easy and congenial fellowship with professed Christians.

The point is clear, is it not, that the tasks of the Christian layman in the world must not only give him his opportunity to fulfil those tasks in the name of Christ (there are some tasks that cannot be performed in Christ's name) but that they must also be used to create for him the opportunities to bear witness to his Master. In other words, every member of the *laos* of God is equally a preacher. But there is this qualification, that while those who are laymen can preach only when they win their chance and their right to do so from those among whom their daily lives are lived, those of us who are preachers by profession suffer from the lack of this handicap. For does not the problem lie here for the professional preacher: that either he has an assured audience, being a minister of a church; or he is able to win his audience by suitable methods of advertisement? How rarely is it recognized that this problem which the non-layman faces is indeed a problem, and that from it arises the serious temptation to look upon the calling of a preacher as simply the call to preach! Those of us whose regular occupation is to preach to Sunday congregations know how, at the end of a service, people come up and shake one's hand and say, "Thank you very much, I enjoyed that sermon." Of course they enjoyed it, for the preacher is their preacher, and they have come to see him perform. I remember, many years ago, preaching at a service in one of our Methodist churches in London. The subject of my sermon was "Hell"; and at the close of the service a lady came to me in the vestry, shook me warmly by the hand, and said, "Thank you very much. I enjoyed that sermon." I looked at her questioningly for a moment, and said, "I did not intend that you should enjoy it." She replied immediately, "I did not. It was awful."

The preacher is not a performer, he is a witness: and somehow a true connection must be established between him and those to whom he witnesses. He must belong to their world and they to his. In the case of the layman, he belongs. His problem is to win his opportunity to speak. In the case of the preacher, the problem is to win his way into the world in which his hearers live. It is said of Father Damien that he began his Sunday sermons to the lepers among whom he lived with these words: "My brethren". One Sunday his opening words were, "We lepers". He had entered their world.

I heard Bishop Lesslie Newbigin say once that the knowledge of God comes to any person never through the skylight but always through the door. "Even the

Jews," he said, "are according to the argument of St. Paul saved in the last analysis by the Gentiles." (Rom. 11: 25–26.) The knowledge of God is always mediated knowledge, one person helping another, and the medium of mediation is the one world to which both belong. "How are men to call upon him in whom they have not believed? And how are they to believe in him of whom they have never heard? And how are they to hear without a preacher? And how can men preach unless they are sent?" (Rom. 10: 14–15)—sent into the world where they must preach, and where they must find themselves as part of it.

At a time in the history of the Church when the meaning and the nature of the sacraments and of the sacramental acts of the Church were the main subjects of theological debate, the doctrine of the priesthood of all believers was hammered out as safeguarding the truth that the Church is one Body. To-day, when the main issue of debate is the nature of the Church and its missionary calling, emphasis falls not on the priest and in what way everyone shares in the Church's priesthood, but on the layman and on the ways in which every believer can discharge his function as a member of the *laos* of God. It was about the unlettered craftsmen of his day that long ago the Son of Sirach wrote: "They will maintain the fabric of the world, and in the handywork of their craft is their prayer." (Ecclus. 38: 34.) The end of God's salvation is a creation re-knit in peace: therefore the instrument of that salvation is a people in fellowship. But that people have no meaning or significance except as they are in the world and for it. They are "salt" which by losing itself preserves the secular and gives it flavour. They are "leaven" which by spreading itself makes the secular serve God's will. They are "light" which by being itself makes God's Kingdom visible in the world. (Matt. 5: 13; 13: 33; 5: 14.)

"The people of God in God's world"—that, then, is the basic fact, and on it depends the nature of every Christian calling. Let me here quote some paragraphs from the Scheme of Church Union in Ceylon.[1]

> The uniting Churches believe that, because the Church is the Body of Christ, it is therefore a royal priesthood through which Christ the risen and ascended High Priest continues His priestly work. All its members are called, in virtue of their union with Christ, to a priestly ministry; both godward, in the offering of spiritual sacrifices, gifts and prayers for mankind; and manward, in the showing forth by life and word of the glory of the redeeming power of God. No individual and no one order in the Church can claim exclusive possession of this priesthood.
>
> . . . . .
>
> The uniting Churches believe that every member of the Church is bound, in virtue of his living member-ship of the Body of Christ, to take his share in the life of the worshipping Church by participating in the worship of the Church on the Lord's Day after the manner of the Apostolic Church, by giving of his substance for the support of the Church and ministry, by witnessing to his faith in his life and daily conduct, and by seeking to bring others into discipleship to Jesus Christ.
>
> . . . . .
>
> It shall be the constant concern of the Church of Lanka to see that the laity make their full contribution in the life of the Church, not merely in the steward-ship of the Church's temporal affairs, but as a lay

[1] Third Revised Edition, pp. 16, 17, 44, 31 (Lutterworth Press).

apostolate which shares in the many-sided encounter with the world wherein lie the Church's evangelistic task and opportunity.

. . . . .

The final victory over sin is God's and it is assured, but it is the privilege of every child of God by his acts of obedience and faith to set up signs which point to that coming victory.

All this adds up to one simple truth, a truth which St. Paul states in straightforward fashion in his letter to the Colossians where he says, "You were called in the one Body to the peace of Christ. Let that peace rule in your hearts. And be thankful." (Cf. Col. 3: 15.) The wholeness which is in Christ, His *Shalom*, belongs to the Church as a whole, and every member of that body in fulfilling his own particular responsibility and vocation is also fulfilling his calling to share in and be an expression of that peace. Actually, there is only one witness to Christ and that is the witness of the Holy Spirit. The witness of Christians is but a witness to His witness. He indwells the Church and gives it gifts in order that with those gifts the Church may witness to Him. "Be my witnesses," said Jesus to His disciples; "but first wait until the Holy Spirit is come into the world and upon you." (Acts 1: 8; cf. John 7: 39.) So do we all receive our calling in the one Body to the peace of Christ, and so are we also called to extend that peace.

For not only is this peace of Christ that to which we are called, it is also that for which our call came. Our Christian discipleship in the world is in order that God's peace may become ruling fact in the lives of individual men and women and in all human affairs. Therefore, says St. Paul, "let the peace of Christ rule in your hearts", for unless you yourselves are subject to that rule you cannot fulfil your calling. "And," he adds, "be thankful." Let your whole life be lived in constant and glad response to this peace that God has established in Christ for you and for all mankind. Thus, when you are unable, for instance, to bring Christ's peace into a particular life or into a particular situation, do not lose heart but learn to give thanks. Remember that peace has already been established in Christ and that, sooner or later, it will swallow up that lack of peace which is your present problem. A baby in its mother's arms is at peace even when it is crying most bitterly. So that, when it is crying, it is as important to remember that it is in its mother's arms as it is to wonder how one may dry its tears.

The wholeness of the body, then, in which all of us who belong to Christ have our calling, and the peace of Christ which is that wholeness, must determine the way in which we understand the specific calling of the preacher. The preacher cannot merely say: I am called to preach, that is my function. Rather, he must learn to say: I am called to be a preacher, I must so conduct my ministry of preaching that it is seen as belonging to the more inclusive ministry of the whole body, a ministry that proceeds from peace to peace. A preacher cannot preach the peace that is in Christ and say at the same time: My task is to preach, but that man's task is to serve in the hospital. Instead, he has himself to share in his brother's work as a doctor by learning so to preach that his message illuminates what the doctor is doing. The reverse is equally true, that the work of the doctor is so to serve in his hospital that he provides proof of the consequences of the Gospel which the preacher is proclaiming. There are many gifts and many callings but one body, so that each calling has to become a particular way in which the peace of the whole body exists and is expressed.

"The mission compound" is one of those institutions in the lands of the younger churches which it has become common to-day to condemn. But in its day it served one very rich purpose. It brought together into a common life the missionary, the local pastor, the doctor, the teacher, the nurse, the sweeper, and made that life the witness of the Church to Christ. The dependence of the mission compound on the control of the Holy Spirit was an inescapable dependence, a situation which we are recovering through the establishment of Ashrams and the founding of Christian communities. It is when one learns to live in community that the work of each arises from and is dependent on the shared life of all. It is in community that the hand learns not to say to the foot, "I do not need you to work with"; and the foot learns not to say to the hand, "I do not need you to walk with." (Cf. 1 Cor. 12: 14–29.)

St. Peter, in his speech in the house of Cornelius, describes the preacher's message as "the good news of peace by Jesus Christ". Here the emphasis falls not on the world from which the preacher comes but on the world to which he comes. It is a world into which Jesus Christ has already entered and, therefore, a world in which everything is falling into place. Jew and Gentile never belonged together, but St. Peter found that the peace of Christ encompassed both. Indeed, it is a wonderful thing to see how, within its very first three decades, the Christian Church and its preachers successfully challenged the forms of peace of their world. Jews and Gentiles, parents and children, husbands and wives, men and women, masters and slaves, rulers and subjects: stern and strong rules had been established regulating all these relationships. But the Church broke through them all in the name of Christ. "Blessed are the peace-makers," said Jesus, "the men who turn the world upside down, for they shall be called the sons of God." (Cf. Matt. 5: 9; Acts 17: 6.) "For what the world gives is not peace, nor do I give peace as the world gives it. In the world, peace is a party cry, it divides; My peace destroys and builds up." Yes, every false form of peace must be destroyed that the Prince of peace may have His way; His way—not only in destroying every false relation but in building up that peace in the world which at His coming the angels proclaimed and for the establishment of which He rules. "You know," says St. Peter to Cornelius, "you know the word which he sent to Israel, preaching good news of peace by Jesus Christ—He is Lord of all."

I was told by a group of teachers, once, about a course they had attended on art and drawing. They said that at the end of a demonstration lesson in which the instructor had shown them how to teach young children to draw, he had asked the little ones to come up to the blackboard and each put some mark on it. Some came up and drew lines, others drew circles and ovals, some just put any kind of mark. And then the instructor took a piece of blue chalk and drew a line horizontally across the board. He began to shade the part beneath the line in blue. He took a piece of green chalk and used it over the lines the children had drawn. He coloured some of the circles and ovals in green and some in pink and red. Some of the marks, just made at random, were touched with white or black: and soon the children saw taking shape on the blackboard a

beautiful lotus pond. There were the green stalks above
and beneath the water, the green leaves spread out on
it, and pink and red lotuses. Above the pond were
wisps of cloud and flying birds. "God," says St. Peter
to Cornelius, "has drawn a blue line across human
history and soon we shall see all things fall into place,
for He is Lord of all. And you too have your place,
even though you are a Gentile, for God's peace through
Jesus Christ includes you as it does all mankind."

> And art Thou come with us to dwell,
> Our Prince, our Guide, our Love, our Lord?
> And is Thy name Emmanuel,
> God present with His world restored?
>
> The world is glad for Thee! The rude
> Wild moor, the city's crowded pen;
> Each waste, each peopled solitude,
> Becomes a home for happy men.
>
> Thy reign eternal will not cease;
> Thy years are sure, and glad, and slow;
> Within Thy mighty world of peace
> The humblest flower hath leave to blow.[1]

"Peace"—that is the determining truth of the
preacher's calling.

> *It determines his message.* He has to proclaim
> to the world that there is peace by Jesus
> Christ.
>
> *It determines his status.* He has to be, as a
> preacher, an expression of the peace of
> Christ in the one body.
>
> *It determines his duty.* He has to find that
> peace to which Jesus calls him in the
> world to which he goes.

[1] Dora Greenwell (Methodist Hymn Book, 259).

The major consideration of these lectures will be directed to this last concern. We shall be seeking to discover, or at least to glimpse, what it does mean for one's daily life in the world that one has dedicated oneself to the task of being a preacher. How does the preacher find that peace to which Jesus calls him in the world to which he is sent? The answer to this question which we shall endeavour to spell out will be that *the calling of a preacher is the calling to be a servant.*

But before we get down to that, there is still another question at which we must look concerning the work of preaching itself; a question on whose answer will depend also our understanding of the nature of the preacher's calling. The question is this: What is preaching, and where does its authority and urgency lie?

Simply because preaching is so often understood as preaching in church on Sundays, or as "revival" preaching to those who are well within the penumbra of the Christian tradition, some of the radical questions which evangelistic preaching raises are not seen in their relation to the work of preaching as a whole. And yet, is it not true that all true preaching is evangelistic preaching, preaching both to the believer and to the unbeliever (and often both are the same person whether one is preaching to Christians or non-Christians), and that, therefore, we shall gain immeasurably in depth in our understanding of the preaching ministry if we face the kind of questions which the task of evangelism poses? To ask "What is preaching, and where does its authority and urgency lie?" is really to ask, "What is evangelism and why must we evangelize?" May I suggest, therefore, that for the rest of this address we use the word "evangelize" interchangeably with the word "preach" and thereby help ourselves to see preaching in the context of the world in which it is actually set.

The first thing to say about evangelism is that it is not a separable activity of the Church or of the Christian. How often do we find that, when a conference on evangelism is convened, within ten minutes people are talking about audio-visual aids? A discussion of evangelistic methods certainly has its own validity, but evangelism itself is not some particular kind of activity. Evangelism happens when God uses anything we do in order to bring people to Him in Jesus Christ. It is a dimension of the Church's total life and, therefore, not an activity that can be separately labelled. Is it not precisely because preaching can be a separable activity that preachers are in danger of treating it as separate? And when this is done, preaching ceases to be the whole Church engaged in proclamation. We evangelize not because it is an activity in which we can choose to engage, but because being in Christ we are inevitably involved in the task of evangelism. We have been raised with Him from the dead through the power of the Holy Spirit and, therefore, find ourselves involved in His continuing ministry in the world. The evangelist is not serving a Lord who has committed a task to him and then departed; rather, he is working with His Lord because he is already in Him. Jesus Christ is the Evangelist, the Apostle. (Heb. 3: 1.) And, because this is true, it is also true that Jesus Christ is previous to the preacher in the lives of those who have still to be brought to Him. They are within His saving ministry. He is already and always at work with them. They have died in Him because He died for them (2 Cor. 5: 14), and they will remain dead unless they are also raised with Him. That this resurrection should happen is what all preaching is about.

We have said that the whole life of the Church is involved in evangelism, and that is the second fact about the nature of evangelism that we must underline. Whether we are talking about the Church's proclamation, or about the Church's task of prophecy—of telling the world what God is doing with it—or about the Church's service to the world, or about its worship or its fellowship, we are talking about evangelism.

Last year when I visited the United States of America I made a new discovery. I found that there fellowship was a verb and not a noun. They talk of fellowshipping with one another. In the New Testament, fellowship is a noun which comes down from heaven. The early disciples found that they were in fellowship—Jew and Gentile, Greek and barbarian, bondman and freeman, male and female. By themselves they could not achieve it, often they did not want it, but they simply found that it was given to them and that they were under compulsion to maintain it and live by it. To-day, when we fellowship with one another, we seek out the people we like either because they hold the same theology, or belong to the same class, or have the right colour. The result is not a Church but a mutual admiration society. We need to learn again from the New Testament to seek and to receive that fellowship which comes as a gift and a compulsion, remembering that where this is missing even worship and sacraments lose their meaning.

The worship of the Church is doxological and doxology has no meaning apart from the witness of the community. (Rom. 12: 1-2.) The rite of baptism has no meaning apart from the task to which it leads and for which the Holy Spirit is given. (Acts 1: 8.) The service of Holy Communion is a proclamation of His death until He come (1 Cor. 11: 26), so that, when there is no intention so to proclaim, the Holy Communion loses its significance. Every activity of the Church's life finds meaning in terms of the evangelistic dimension within which the Church lives and, in turn, this evangelistic dimension gives meaning to the Church's every activity. Preaching is but one instrument in a great orchestra.

The question which we raised and to which we have sought an answer was, "What is preaching and where does its authority and urgency lie?" Or, "What is evangelism and why must we evangelize?" We have indicated something of an answer to the first part of the question: What is preaching? Let us now turn to the second part—where does its authority and urgency lie?

In raising this question of authority, we from Asia usually have a different set of questions in mind from the questions that you in the West will naturally raise. A few months ago, I received a letter from a missionary friend of mine asking my advice as to what to do in the case of a young Muslim, son of a doctor, who in the university had decided to become a Christian. If he went back home the boy felt that he would be forced into a Muslim marriage, if he stayed away from home it would probably be a decision to stay away from his home permanently. He had to choose between his parents and Jesus Christ. Some years ago I baptized a young man whose sister had sought baptism earlier. He wanted to join his sister in the religion she professed because he was drawn to it by her faith and example. To-day, that young man is married to his first cousin, a Hindu. It was a marriage that had all along been intended by the parents on both sides and from which the young man could not get free. He must now take his wife, and leave her parents' home and find a house to live in, in the midst of a Christian community so that the wife may find herself free to go to church, to receive Christian instruction and, in time, be baptized. But the wife cannot leave her parents so easily, because they are old and the father is an invalid.

You can see the implication of what I am saying. In our part of the world, the preacher, the evangelist, is engaged in the work of disrupting people's lives. And so the question must be asked, "By what authority does he do it?" Again and again I have found, in conferences and conversations on evangelism, that when this issue of authority is raised many give this kind of answer. "Jesus has done this for me. He can do the same for them. I must tell them." Is that sufficient authority to disrupt somebody's life? Or, some people say, "The Church needs to evangelize. Our own Christian life and its nurture depend upon it." That may be true, but why engage in an activity where it is somebody else who has to pay the price? And still others base their authority on the great commission: "Go into all the world and preach the Gospel to the whole creation." (Mk. 16: 15; cf. Matt. 28: 18–20.) Here is a command that must be obeyed. True, but how is it that neither in the Acts of the Apostles nor in the epistles is this command quoted as constituting the evangelist's authority? In fact, what we find in the Acts of the Apostles and the epistles is an answer to this question not in terms of what God has done for the evangelist but in terms of what God has done for the world; not in terms of a command to be obeyed but in terms of an inner necessity to be accepted. God has loved the world in Jesus Christ, and Jesus Christ is at work seeking to bring the world into obedience to the Father, so that they who are members of Christ find themselves sharing in Christ's ministry. Their authority lies not in the fact that Jesus has entered their lives but in the fact that they have entered His. The crux of the difficulty is here that the preacher thinks of himself as taking Jesus to those who know Him not, when the truth is that it is Jesus who is taking the preacher to bear witness to Him. The preacher is the gift, Jesus is the giver. Jesus said to His disciples, "Go, wait; when you receive the Holy Spirit you shall be my witnesses" (Acts 1: 8) and the disciples found that this was so. They found in the compulsion of the Holy Spirit both their authority and their enabling power. He took them and gave them to the world.

The question of authority is immediately linked with the question of urgency. In the early years of the modern missionary movement, this urgency was stated in terms of the certainty that those who in this life did not accept Jesus as Saviour would be damned. People were going to hell and they must be given their chance to believe in Jesus Christ. The matter was urgent. This way of stating the urgency of the evangelistic task is now impossible for most Christians. At the Jerusalem Conference of the International Missionary Council in 1928, it was said that while "our fathers were impressed with the horror that men should die without Christ, we are impressed also with the horror that men should live without Christ".[1] The urgency of the evangelistic task lay in helping people so to find Him that they may live the abundant life that He came to bring. We are now in 1958, thirty years after the Jerusalem Conference.

[1] Jerusalem Meeting Report of the I.M.C. (Vol. I, p. 406).

Can we say that the average performance of the Christian community around the world is any higher than that of the Hindu community, or the Muslim or the Buddhist? To answer that these communities have also been influenced by Christ is to beg the question. For the question is not about the influence which Christianity exerts, but about the demand that it makes that all men, and each man, should believe in Jesus Christ as Saviour and obey Him as Lord. May I make bold to say that in our Christian Churches the problem of un-faith lies precisely here? that, having lost confidence in the ways in which we used to state the necessity for evangelism, we have now ceased to believe in that necessity. We still believe that it is necessary for us to evangelize, but we do not believe that it is necessary for them to be evangelized. When our preaching does not convert we are concerned that we have failed, but there is little sense of loss concerning those who will not hear and believe.

Where did the early disciples find the urgency that drove them around the world they knew, turning it upside down? Is it not true that they found their urgency in the very message they proclaimed? They said that Jesus was risen; that, with the limitations of His flesh removed, He was at work in the world; and they found themselves almost winded keeping pace with Him. He was at work here, there, and everywhere, breaking down and building up, constructing that peace which He came to bring, and they who were in Christ found themselves involved in the same breathless urgency. Jesus is Lord of the world as of the Church, and we can see to-day, more clearly than we have ever seen, the tempo at which events in the world are moving as well as the calamities that happen where the obedience of the Church does not keep pace with these events. What difference would a more urgent obedience to the demands of the Gospel in Asian lands during the last one hundred and fifty years have made to what is happening in Asia to-day in the realm of political and social affairs? What incalculable difference it would make in our countries in Asia in the future if the Churches in these countries would be more alive to what our Lord is doing among our peoples.

Let me give you an example. In Ceylon the so-called lower castes are on the march, aggressively on the march. Jesus is leading them to freedom. I said two years ago to one of our Christian educational governing bodies in Jaffna that we must take steps immediately to employ teachers in our schools from among these castes. Except one of my ministerial colleagues in that committee, nobody would support me. They were afraid about the reaction of the high-caste Hindus whose children are also in our schools. They were afraid of the reaction of the high-caste teachers in our schools, both Hindu and Christian. Now, within two years, we are finding that the situation has got out of hand. These so-called out-castes are building their own schools under Hindu auspices, employing their own teachers, and the Christian Church is left behind to do what it likes. It is when the Church learns to obey the Lord of the world that it will discover where the urgency of its task lies.

In 1952, at the Faith and Order Conference at Lund, a message was issued calling upon the Churches "to act together in all matters except those in which deep differences of conviction compel them to act separately".[1] It is 1958 now. Can we say that this word from Lund has made any difference? Is it not true that

[1] Report of the Third World Conference on Faith and Order, p. 6.

still, as Confessions and Denominations, we are committed to the position that we shall do everything separately except those things which the world forces us to do together? And when the world does so force us, we find often that we are already too late. I heard somewhere the story of a missionary who went to China some years ago. When he arrived, his friend who met him at the airport said to him, "You have arrived in the nick of time." To which he replied, "When I came here for the first time seven years ago, I was told then that I had arrived in the nick of time." "Well," said his friend, "time is getting nicker every day."

In the last discourse of our Lord as recorded in St. Mark's gospel (Mk. 13) He spoke to His disciples about the world. "The world must suffer," He said, "therefore you will suffer also. The world will make you suffer." "The world must be judged," He said, "therefore you too will be judged. The world will be the instrument of your judgment." "The world must see the Christ," He said, "therefore you must proclaim Him. The world itself will force you to do this by proclaiming false christs." "The world must be harvested," He said, "therefore you must work for that harvest. For the gospel must first be preached to all nations before the end comes."

The World, the Gospel, the Church—and all three belonging together in that peace which Christ has established; that is the reality within which the preaching ministry is exercised.

The Gospel is preached that men may believe and be saved. The Gospel is preached that men may find in it the possibility of the life abundant. But the urgency of the preacher's task is not in what he thinks about the nature of that task but in the task itself. It has a momentum apart from him and he is either carried by that momentum or is disobedient. The question is not whether he can state why the task is urgent but whether he finds it so. The question is not whether he can state what his authority is but whether he knows himself as an instrument of the Lord's authority. The calling of a preacher is not simply a call to preach, with his task to be understood in terms of preaching as such. Rather, the calling of a preacher is like every Christian calling, a call to share in the continuing ministry of the risen and ascended Lord. The Lord is Servant and we are His servants set to serve the world, so that the preaching ministry like every ministry of the Church is consequent on this servant-hood or it declares itself illegitimate.

[1] There were two men who lived on the King's highway; one was poor and the other rich. The poor man lived by the work of his own hands, while the rich man lived by the work of other men's hands. One day a messenger came bidding each man prepare to receive the King, who was coming that way.

The rich man looked out of the window of his house. He could see the great road winding away in the distance, for he lived at the top of the hill which overlooked the valley; and he saw at the foot of the hill the cottage of the poor man. "I wonder," he said to himself, "what a poor creature such as he can do to receive a King. With all my wealth and slaves I can build such a temple as men have never seen, but what can that fellow do? Whatever he does will be worse than useless."

So the rich man began to build. His slaves toiled all day long and far into the nights, until a vast temple rose on the top of the hill. The gates were of gold, and the great dome was starred with costly gems, while the

[1] From *Day Dreams*, by Reginald J. Barker (Epworth Press).

massive pillars were cased in silver. The floor and walls were of white marble. In the centre of the temple stood a throne cushioned with soft crimson velvet, and studded with diamonds. Beneath the arched roof, and between the pillars, golden censers were hanging, in which costly incense burned. When it was finished the rich man rubbed his hands with glee, saying to himself, "Nothing can compare with this in the whole wide world."

Meanwhile the poor man had purchased bricks and timber with his hard-earned savings. He went without food in order to have money to spend. All day he was out toiling for his living; and then half the night— sometimes the whole night—he worked at his little chapel. At last it was finished. It was quite unadorned and lowly. Within, the walls were whitewashed, and the wooden floor was spotlessly clean. There was a small table covered with a plain crimson cloth for an altar; a chair—the best one out of his house; a rude though carefully carved cross upon the table; and two metal candlesticks holding wax candles. It was simple, but it was all he had.

When the rich man saw the small chapel of the poor man he laughed aloud. "Poor fool!" he cried. "Does he think a King would enter there?" When the poor man saw the marble temple on the hilltop his heart sank, and he said to himself, "He will never enter mine."

The day came. The rich man, richly dressed, stood on the steps of the temple, waiting. Within, a choir of singers waited to chant the welcome to the King. As the rich man stood waiting, he muttered uneasily, "He will never pass me by! It would be an insult to my generosity to go elsewhere. But then there is nowhere else," and he laughed again as he thought of the poor man's chapel.

All day he waited, but the King did not come. As

the day was ending a great storm burst upon the hillside. Lightning flashed and thunder rolled. Suddenly the temple was struck. The walls tottered and the earth shook—and the temple was a ruin.

But the poor man's chapel was unharmed. Early that morning he had entered that chapel and knelt before the altar. "I dare not hope for Thy coming," he prayed. "This house is too simple and lowly; it is unfit for Thy glory. The heart that planned it is sinful, and the hands that made it are stained and soiled. Yet it is all I have. Take it, Lord! Enter or leave it— it is Thine!" He prayed on till eventide. Then as the storm broke upon the hillside, a sudden light filled the shrine. The poor man dared not look up, but he felt the Royal Presence there. Then a voice spoke to him. "I have seen all thy love and sacrifice. I have seen thy tears and heard thy prayer. Lo, I am with you always."

The voice ceased. The light faded. But the poor man's heart was glad with the Presence of the King.

He shows strength with his arm.
He scatters the proud in the imagination of their
    hearts, and exalts those of low degree.
He fills the hungry with good things and the rich
    he sends empty away.
My soul magnifies the Lord,
For he who is mighty has done great things for me,
    and holy is his name.

(Cf. Lk. 1: 46–53.)

Now unto him that is able to do exceeding abundantly above all that we ask or think, according to the power that worketh in us, unto him be the glory in the Church and in Christ Jesus unto all generations for ever and ever. Amen.

(Eph. 3: 20–21, R.V.)

2

You are my trusty witnesses, the servants I have
chosen, to own me, to believe me, to see that I am
ever the same. . . .

I, I am the Eternal, there is no saviour besides me.
'Twas I who promised to save, I who fulfilled what
I foretold . . . you are my trusty witnesses to that.

From of old I am God, and from henceforth the
same; no one can snatch out of my hand, and what
I do no one can reverse.

(Is. 43: 10–13, Moffatt.)

O God, by whom the meek are guided in judgment, and
light riseth up in darkness for the godly; grant us, in our
doubts and uncertainties, the grace to ask what thou
wouldst have us to do; that the Spirit of wisdom may save
us from false choices, and that in thy light we may see light,
and in thy straight path may not stumble; through Jesus
Christ our Lord. Amen.

Prayer by William Bright.

2. The Preacher's Calling to be Servant

For we preach not ourselves, but Christ Jesus as Lord, and ourselves as your servants for Jesus' sake.
(2 Cor. 4: 5, R.V.)

THERE was trouble in the church at Corinth. Controversy had arisen about the relation between moral discipline and Christian belief. There was also a discussion about the nature of the purity of the Christian fellowship and how it was to be maintained. Then the controversy had broadened to include a questioning about the kind of authority the apostle Paul had over the life and decisions of the Corinthian church which he had helped to found. The result of all this was a great deal of confusion of thought and misunderstanding, and factions within the church. Where did responsibility lie for this situation?

St. Paul gives a straight answer. "We speak the plain truth," he says, "and so commend ourselves to every man's conscience in the sight of God. If our gospel is 'veiled', the veil must be in the minds of those who are spiritually dying. The spirit of this world has blinded the minds of those who do not believe, and prevents the light of the glorious gospel of Christ, the image of God, from shining on them. For it is Christ Jesus the Lord Whom we preach, not ourselves; we are your servants for His sake." (2 Cor. 4: 2–5, Phillips' paraphrase.[1])

[1] *Letters to Young Churches*, J. B. Phillips (Macmillan Co.)

St. Paul has no hesitation in denying that any blame attaches to him. "If our Gospel is veiled," he asserts, "the veil must be in the minds of those who are spiritually dying." It is not that the Apostle is unaware of his own human-ness and all his faults and failings. He says quite plainly, "Not that we are sufficient of ourselves to claim anything as coming from us; our sufficiency is from God who has qualified us to be ministers of a new covenant—a treasure we have in earthen vessels." (2 Cor. 3: 5–6; 4: 7.)

In other words, the problem in the Corinthian church was not at bottom a problem caused by differences of opinion and clash of personalities. It was rather a problem caused by unbelief. And with respect to that problem St. Paul could speak with confidence because he could lay claim to two incontestable facts.

> (i) First of all, his preaching had been about Jesus Christ and no one else. "It is Christ Jesus as Lord that I proclaim," [1] he says. Your controversy, therefore, is not about me or with me but actually about Him and with Him. He is your Lord and mine. I did not seek in His name to exercise any lordship over you. You can deal with Him direct. Indeed, you must.
>
> (ii) Secondly, "I am simply a servant of yours for Jesus' sake." [1] He, who is my Lord and whose servant I am, made me your servant. I became a servant "through Him" [2]. He subjugated me and, therefore, just as your controversy is not

---

[1] Moffatt's translation.   [2] R.V. margin.

with me, neither can my controversy be with you. In all my dealings with you, whatever you do to me or say about me, I have still to remain your servant. Jesus made me that, and that I must continue to be. But, "as I hold this ministry by God's mercy to me, I never lose heart in it".[1]

Let me illustrate the significance of the nexus of ideas that arise from this text by sharing with you the way in which this text first laid hold on me. I was preparing an address to be delivered at a missionaries' meeting on "The place and function of the missionary in the Church in Ceylon". I was intending to deal particularly with the problems of indigenization and devolution: problems which were the major issues of discussion at that time. I had chosen this text as a suitable way of expressing the role of the missionary. He had come to preach Jesus Christ and not himself. The local church was, therefore, free to be itself. But, then the second half of the text proved troublesome. It didn't seem right for me to say to the missionaries, "You are our servants through Jesus." Nobody has the right to claim somebody else as servant. . . . Whilst still in the middle of preparing this address, I went to see one of my missionary friends, the Rev. Gilbert Jessop. He had been involved in a conflict with local church leaders. They had wanted certain decisions made in a particular way and he had opposed them decisively. His last words to me at the close of my conversation with him were, "Niles, I am not wanted here but I know I am needed, and so here I mean to stay."

[1] 2 Cor. 4: 1 (Moffatt).

I understood, then, what it really meant to be servant "through Jesus". The missionary was not servant to do what local church leaders demanded of him simply because they demanded it. He had to do what he was convinced Christ demanded of him, because Christ was his Master and Master also of those among whom his service was set. But this was also true, that whether his service was accepted or not, was acceptable or not, he could not quit. "Servant" was what he had been appointed to be, and their servant he had to remain.

Here is the essential nature of the preacher's calling—that we are preachers not because God has called us to be preachers but because God has called us to be servants. When we surrendered ourselves to Him, we surrendered ourselves to become His servants. It was part of the mystery of His will for us that He made us servants to our fellows. We became servants through Him, by His action. And it is right that it should be so. For He himself is Servant, so that we as servants of the Servant can have no other career. "As the Father has sent me, even so I send you" (John 20: 21) were His words of appointment to us. It was as Servant He was sent, it is as servants that we are called.

"Though he was in the form of God, he did not count equality with God a thing to be grasped, but emptied himself, taking the form of a servant, being born in the likeness of men. And being found in human form he humbled himself and became obedient unto death, even death on a cross. Therefore God has highly exalted him." (Phil. 2: 6–9.) There can be little doubt that in this classic passage, which may very well be one of the earliest hymns of the Church, there is conscious reference to the Servant-songs of Isaiah. A Jewish ear would certainly detect in this description of Jesus that earlier description of "the Servant" (53: 11) who "humbled" himself (53: 8), "emptied" his soul unto death (53: 12) and was "highly exalted" (52: 13).[1]

> Behold, my servant shall be exalted and lifted up,
> He shall be very high.
> He was oppressed yet he humbled himself,
> He poured out his soul unto death,
> He was numbered with the transgressors,
> He bore the sin of many.

In a significant incident that took place during His earthly ministry, Jesus himself referred explicitly to His servant-role and set it forward as the pattern which His disciples were to follow. The mother of the sons of Zebedee had asked Him to give her sons special positions in the Kingdom. Jesus granted them the privilege of sharing His cup of suffering and His baptism of death. When the other disciples murmured, He said to them, "Why murmur? Do you not know that whatever anyone's request for position or precedence, all that I will grant is the career of a servant? For the Son of man came not to be served but to serve, and to give his life a ransom for many." (Matt. 20: 20–28.) "He bore the sin of many" (Is. 53: 12) was the Isaianic description of the suffering Servant; so that the allusion to it in this saying of Jesus about the Son of man is a plain one.

The allusion is even plainer in St. Luke's gospel where, in the course of the discussion about precedence and position that takes place during the last supper, He refers directly to the future that awaits Him and

[1] Cf. notes by C. H. Dodd in the *Journal of Theological Studies*, July 1938, p. 292.

speaks of himself, quoting the Servant-song of Isaiah, as one who will be "numbered with the transgressors". (Lk. 22: 37.) "I shall become an outcast," He says to His disciples, "and you must be prepared to share with me my outcast destiny."

In St. John's gospel, Jesus deals with the controversy among His disciples about place and position by arising from supper and, having girded himself with a towel, washing His disciples' feet. Commenting on this incident the evangelist says, "Jesus, knowing that the Father had given all things into his hands, and that he had come from God and was going to God, rose from supper, laid aside his garments, and girded himself with a towel." (John 13: 3-4.) The garments of the Master are laid by, He takes the form of a servant. As servant He came from God, as servant He must return to God; there is for Him no remission of the servant's tasks.

In a saying of Jesus recorded in St. Luke in the course of his narrative about the last supper, this incident of washing the disciples' feet finds an echo. Jesus says to His disciples, "Let the greatest among you become as the youngest, and the leader as one who serves. For which is the greater, one who sits at table, or one who serves? Is it not the one who sits at table? But I am among you as one who serves." (Lk. 22: 26-27.) And here the Western text beautifully adds, "and you have grown, while I waited upon you, to be like the servant".[1]

How wonderfully comforting that truth is: He serves, and as He waits upon us we too become servants like Him. "I will make you" (Mk. 1: 17) is His promise, and on that promise we rely as we seek to fulfil our calling. We are called to be servants, called to share in

[1] See critical apparatus, Nestlé's text of the Greek New Testament, Stuttgart edition, 1920.

46

and continue the servant-ministry of the Christ. To speak of the Church as an extension of the Incarnation is to make too close an identification of the Church with Christ's person, but to speak of the Church as an extension of His ministry is to make a true identification of the Church with His work. The Body of Christ is the Christ present in His on-going work. Of that Body we are members.

> The kingdoms of the earth go by
>   In purple and in gold;
> They rise, they flourish, and they die,
>   And all their tale is told.

> One Kingdom only is Divine,
>   One banner triumphs still,
> Its King a servant, and its sign
>   A gibbet on a hill.[1]

Here lies the explanation of St. Paul's characteristic description of himself as "a servant of Jesus Christ". Whenever he refers to his apostleship, he always adds a phrase such as "by the will of God" (1 Cor. 1: 1) or "by command of God" (1 Tim. 1: 1); but when he speaks of himself as servant that description stands alone. That is what he essentially is. To use his own words, found in his epistle to the Romans, he is "a servant of Jesus Christ, called to be an apostle". (Rom. 1: 1.) St. Paul cannot forget how he was mastered on his way to Damascus by Jesus Christ. Jesus was already master then, His yoke was upon Paul; but Paul was rebelling against that mastery. Jesus said to him, "You are my servant: my yoke is upon you and if you rebel it is only yourself that you will hurt." (Cf. Acts 26: 14.) So St. Paul discovered his master, and

[1] G. F. Bradby.

47

so learned to give his neck to his master's yoke until he found that yoke easy and its burden light. (Matt. 11: 30.) In no other circumstance but as servant of Jesus Christ could proud St. Paul have learned to say, "I have made myself a slave to all, I have become all things to all men." (1 Cor. 9: 19, 22.) "I am become and am now a doormat[1] on whom all wipe their feet." (1 Cor. 4: 13.)

Or, let us look for a moment at St. Peter. His whole life had been lived according to the social code of his people, but now he was being asked to accept a Gentile, Cornelius, as his brother in Christ. Peter knew enough about Jesus Christ to know that the acceptance of Cornelius as his brother would have to be a total acceptance. He had a simple mind incapable of the casuistry (or what has come to be called nowadays the historical perspective) which we, for instance, in Ceylon find so useful in enabling us to live with a good conscience alongside the caste system, or which you in the West find so useful in maintaining colonial or racial attitudes. Peter saw quite clearly that there was only one way of accepting the Gentiles as his brethren and that was to be willing to become their servant for Christ's sake. Peter obeyed because Jesus mastered him. (Acts 10: 9–20.) "Rise and go down," the Master said, and for Peter there was no alternative but to obey. As he explained to some of his Jewish friends later, "Who was he that he could withstand God?" (Acts 11: 17.)

Obedience is what the word "servant" primarily suggests, even though to a modern ear it may suggest employment, wages, contract. To those who heard the word in the time of St. Paul or St. Peter, it simply

[1] In the Dutch Bible, the phrase used to translate 1 Cor. 4: 13 literally means "that on which all wipe their feet".

brought to mind a picture of the slave-market. The slave was bought and owned by his master. He was at his master's disposal. Whatever good the slave received from his master was of pure grace, he had no rights; and as for his labour it earned him no rewards. Is it not because we have so little emotional understanding of what it means to be a slave that we also find it so difficult to understand what the Scriptures tell us about the wonder of God's grace? It is only a slave who knows that he is a slave who can also know the unaccountable joy of being the slave of a gracious master. Is it any surprise that the contemporaries of that first Christian community were puzzled by this Christian joy at having a master, a master who could demand of them even death in His service, and yet whom in the hour of death they could salute with hymns of joy? "It seems to me," says St. Paul, "that God means us apostles to come in at the very end, like the doomed gladiators in the arena!" (1 Cor. 4: 9, Moffatt.)

"Servants of Jesus Christ", "Servants through Jesus Christ", "Servants for Christ's sake": those, then, are the preacher's credentials. That is what he is: servant to the Lord to whom he owes obedience, and servant to his fellows to whom he owes his service. "The freedom to which we are called," said St. Paul, "is freedom through love to be servants of one another." "Do not use your freedom," he warned, "to bite and devour one another lest you be consumed by one another." (Gal. 5: 13–15.) David Livingstone, towards the close of his long pilgrimage as servant, bore this testimony to Jesus Christ:

> He is the greatest Master I have ever known. If there is anyone greater I do not know him. Jesus Christ is the only Master supremely worth serving. He is the

only ideal that never loses its inspiration. He is the only friend whose friendship meets every demand. He is the only Saviour who can save us to the uttermost. We go forth in His name, in His power, and in His Spirit, to serve Him.

We can desire to make no less a discovery of Jesus Christ, but the condition of that discovery is the same for us as for Livingstone. It is servanthood without the possibility either of escaping or of being excused from it. St. Paul, who had been appointed by Christ to be servant to the Christian church at Corinth, states quite plainly what this servanthood had meant to him and to them. He says in his letter, "We are made a public spectacle before the angels of Heaven and the eyes of man. We are looked upon as fools, for Christ's sake, but you are wise in the Christian faith. We are considered weak, but you have become strong: you have found honour, we little but contempt. . . . Men curse us, but we return a blessing: they make our lives miserable but we take it patiently. They ruin our reputations but we go on trying to win them for God. We are the world's rubbish, the scum of the earth, yes, up to this very day." (1 Cor. 4: 9–13, Phillips' paraphrase.[1])

It is out of this experience that St. Paul speaks when he reminds his friends in Corinth of the message he had preached among them. "We preached," he says, "Jesus Christ as Lord, with ourselves as your servants through Jesus." "Jesus with ourselves"—the two belong together as parts of one theme. It is not possible to preach Jesus Christ as Lord unless the preacher can also witness to having been made a servant to others through Jesus; nor is it possible to be a servant to others except as part of one's testimony to the lordship of Jesus Christ. The

[1] *Letters to Young Churches* (Macmillan Co.)

two facts belong together and, for the preacher, arise out of a single event, an event which St. Paul describes in its simplicity in these words: "He loved me and gave himself for me." (Gal. 2: 20.) I am no more mine but His, and that event in which He purchased His slave is also the event in which the slave found a Master in whom he could rejoice. The preaching of the slave is the result of that joy.

In the well-known conversion hymn of the Wesleys is a fine example of this connection between the call of the servant, the task of the preacher, and the joy of the redeemed.

> Where shall my wondering soul begin?
>   How shall I all to heaven aspire?
> A slave redeemed from death and sin,
>   A brand plucked from eternal fire,
> How shall I equal triumphs raise,
> Or sing my great Deliverer's praise?
>
> And shall I slight my Father's love?
>   Or basely fear His gifts to own?
> Unmindful of His favours prove?
>   Shall I, the hallowed cross to shun,
> Refuse His righteousness to impart,
> By hiding it within my heart?[1]

Saved by grace, the Wesleys find themselves lifted by joy and engaged as preachers. But they know the subtle temptation to refuse to preach in order that the preacher may avoid the cross that inevitably belongs to the experience of the servant.

> Shall I, the hallowed cross to shun,
> Refuse His righteousness to impart,
> By hiding it within my heart?

[1] Charles Wesley.

That is clear discernment of what it means for a preacher to be called with the calling of a servant. For it is not merely to the service of preaching that one is called, but rather to be servant to those to whom one preaches. Indeed, the accent falls not on any particular service that one is able or is enabled to render, but rather on one's own status as a servant. It is damnably easy to serve—there are always those to whom we can dole out our service—but it is not so easy to be a servant. St. Paul found that to be a servant was to be at the mercy of those whom he was set to serve, and yet not quite, for he belonged to Jesus Christ. "We are afflicted in every way," he wrote, "but not crushed; perplexed, but not driven to despair; persecuted, but not forsaken; struck down, but not destroyed; always carrying in the body the death of Jesus. But thanks be to God, who in Christ always leads us in triumph, and through us spreads the fragrance of the knowledge of him everywhere. For we are the aroma of Christ to God." (2 Cor. 4: 8–10; 2: 14–15.)

Jesus loved men when they desired not to be so loved, and because His love was so persistent and so demanding men killed Him on a cross. The cross was the price of love. To-day when men suffer for the truth or for justice we speak of them as sharing the cross. In a sense that is so. And yet, how different it is when one suffers because one loves. When, at Caesarea Philippi, Jesus asked His disciples who men thought He was, one of the answers was that they thought He was Jeremiah. (Matt. 16: 14.) That was a tribute to that tender prophet who had loved his people and who because he loved them had suffered for them at their hands. The servant cannot run away, because he is servant through Jesus Christ; but because he cannot run away, and will not let go those whom he is set to serve, he is led everywhere in triumph spreading the fragrance of a flower that is crushed.

When John the Baptist sent messengers to Jesus asking, "Are you he who is to come?" the reply of Jesus was in terms of His credentials as Servant. "Go and tell John," He said, "what you hear and see: the blind receive their sight and the lame walk, lepers are cleansed and the deaf hear, and the dead are raised up, and the poor have good news preached to them." (Matt. 11: 3–5.) The deeds which the Servant is able to perform are the manifest signs of the power of the Kingdom that has come. So it shall be with us too who are preachers. "For we are his workmanship, created in Christ Jesus for good works, which God prepared beforehand, that we should walk in them." (Eph. 2: 10.) In the words with which the ending of St. Mark's gospel closes, "They went forth and preached everywhere, while the Lord worked with them and confirmed the message by the signs that attended it." (Mk. 16: 20.)

To-day we are witnessing a revival of understanding that is taking place in many ways of the preacher's calling to be servant. Among these there are two of increasing importance. There is, on the one hand, a growing awareness of the true nature and authority of the pastoral ministry and, on the other hand, there is the growing attempt on the part of the ordained ministers of the Church to get closer to the servants of the world—the workers—to meet them and serve them where they are. Of course, it was always accepted that a minister of the Gospel was a servant of the people, but what is now becoming clear is that there is a fundamental difference between serving and being a servant. Jesus said to His disciples, "Look at the Gentiles. It is the bosses among them who are called benefactors. Let it not be so with you." (Cf. Lk. 22: 25–26.) Benefactors are bureaucrats. A bureaucrat is also engaged in service but he himself is not a servant but a boss.

The Church exists to serve, but there is always the problem of preserving the servant-attitude of the institutions which the Church creates as the means of its service. These institutions can so easily become vested interests, with the result that those responsible for the working of these institutions become servants not of the people whom the institutions are designed to serve but of the institutions themselves. In our part of the world, in Asia, this danger is fraught with great consequence for those of us who are ordained ministers of the Church. For, as conditions are there, it is the ordained ministry which in large measure is also involved in the governing bodies of the Church's institutions such as hospitals, schools, orphanages, community centres; so that when these institutions become vested interests of the Church, that is, when they are looked upon as those expressions of the Church's life and activity which it must protect in order to preserve its own secular power and influence, then the ordained ministry itself inevitably tends to become a bureaucracy. And once this happens, the whole relation of the minister with the people is poisoned.

It is only now that it is being slowly realized in the younger churches of Asia that both for the sake of the service-institutions of our churches as well as for the sake of their ordained ministry it is essential that these institutions should cease to be ecclesiastically and centrally controlled. They must become true expressions of the Church's lay-life, of the fact that the people of God live primarily as part of the world. It was one thing, for instance, for the Methodist Church in Ceylon to have had a unified administration during the time that it was still under the control of the British Methodist Missionary Society; it is quite another thing for the Methodist Church in Ceylon now to bring under one governing authority all expressions of its life, and especially those expressions of its life as servant in the world.

This possibility of serving without being a servant can arise, however, not only with respect to the service-institutions of the Church; it can arise also in the way in which the Church's stewardship of the mysteries of God is discharged. (1 Cor. 4: 1.) A young missionary who came to work in the Church in Ceylon left us and returned to his home because he felt compelled to do things that he did not want to do. His only task, he said, was to preach the Gospel. He was certainly an effective preacher, but his congregation did not need a benefactor of God's word but a servant. Even with respect to the sacraments, how often they are made the mark of the priest, distinguishing him from his people, instead of being the sign of the priesthood of the whole people of God! Servanthood: that, then, is the crux of the matter; and the preacher who is not a servant becomes a benefactor.

We said that there were two significant ways in which there is to-day a revival of understanding of this call of the preacher to be a servant, and that one of them is a growing awareness of the true nature and authority of the pastoral ministry. The pastoral ministry has always been recognized as an integral part of the preacher's calling but not always has the connection between the two been truly assessed. The pastor is at the service of his people, but it is not they who engaged him. He is not a kind of personnel-officer appointed by the community and paid by them in order that he may fulfil certain community duties. The pastor is simply an under-shepherd of the great Shepherd, who asks him just one question before he is appointed, "Do you love me?"; and if the answer be "Yes", then gives him his commission: "Feed my sheep." (John 21: 17.)

The pastoral function issues from and is sustained by two relationships—the pastor's love for his Master, and the Master's love for His sheep. The pastor will often find it difficult to love the sheep but he can have no difficulty in loving the Master; the sheep may often succeed in refusing their pastor's ministry but they will never succeed in preventing their Master's love. In other words, it is on the truth that Jesus Christ is Lord that the pastoral ministry is dependent and, therefore, it is by the proclamation of this truth that the pastoral ministry is safeguarded.

In that classic passage in the book of Ezekiel (chapter 34) where the Great Shepherd speaks to His under-shepherds, how significantly the emphasis falls on the activity of the Great Shepherd himself and the control He exercises over the pastoral ministry that He has ordained for His sheep. If the shepherds should devour the sheep, then the Great Shepherd will be against them. If the sheep should quarrel amongst themselves, then the Great Shepherd will judge between them. Where any sheep are lost, the Great Shepherd himself will find them. Where wild beasts attack the sheep, the Great Shepherd himself will protect them. Is it not well that this is so? For, think what the situation must be if we human beings should be left alone and to one another; if service to ensure human welfare should be made dependent on man's love for man because God had either been abandoned or outlawed! With what intensity would we then work for one another because there would be no possibility of working for God; or with what decisiveness would we harm one another because there would be no one to prevent us or protect us? Are we not, in fact, already witnessing the tremendous power both for good and for evil which the love of man for man can generate when it is divorced from the love of God?

> The love of man for man's sake [says a perceptive Christian writer] must necessarily be stronger and richer in other camps than ours. Are they not confined within a world from which heaven has been removed like a roof? On the level floor of a plain visible from end to end, objects stand out stark and bare, hopeless captives of the relentless light which has stripped them of every wonder, every blessed dream. And on such an earth, without cover or distance, when longing reaches into the void, these people are packed unendurably tight, treading on each other's feet, too close to escape. These people, who have nothing but themselves, who are without God, how terribly important they must become to one another—important as we who live simultaneously and inseparably with God can never be important to each other![1]

It is well, it is indeed well both for the sheep and for the shepherds that the condition of the pastoral calling is the love which the shepherds bear to the Great Shepherd of all and not the love which they bear to the sheep. The sheep the shepherds must love and that love

[1] Ida F. Coudenhove, *The Nature of Sanctity* (Sheed and Ward, Ltd.), pp. 96–97.

they must learn, but their love for the Great Shepherd is their standing ground.

"It is Jesus Christ who is Lord while we are your servants through Jesus." So said St. Paul. We are your servants, but Jesus Christ is Lord, both your Lord and ours. So that, while we owe service to you, it is to Him that we render our account. You never become the lord of the servants He sends you. The sheep and the shepherds belong to one another through the Great Shepherd and never directly. St. Paul, in his first letter to the Corinthians, had already written to them and said, "It matters very little to me what you, or any man, thinks of me—I don't even value my opinion of myself. For I might be quite ignorant of any fault in myself—but that doesn't justify me before God. My only true judge is God himself." (1 Cor. 4: 3, 4, Phillips' paraphrase.[1]) That being so, how evident it becomes that a preacher's whole ministry, even his pastoral ministry, depends on what he preaches. Let him have doubts or reservations about the Lordship of Jesus Christ and he will become a social-service agent in the community. The people will still come to hear him preach, but it will be because, from their point of view, he preaches "helpful" sermons, and because he is "their" preacher. The preacher loses his status as "servant through Jesus" unless his lips proclaim that "Jesus is Lord". The preacher is bound up with the message he proclaims.

But there is also the converse of this truth, that however true one's message may be it needs to be rooted in a servant's life. My second son when he was a little boy said to me one day, "Papa, I want to be a preacher when I grow up." I asked him why. His answer was,

[1] *Letters to Young Churches* (Macmillan Co.)

58

pointing to the pulpit in my church where this conversation took place, "I want to stand inside that and tell everybody what they must do." He was choosing the preacher's role without knowing what it meant to be servant.

One of the chief weaknesses of many of us Christians, I would say, is our inability to think theologically about our daily problems. We have a fair theological understanding of the Christian faith, but when it comes to daily living our approach to our problems is largely in terms of "good conduct" and a "this-worldly prudence". I have often wondered whether this general weakness may not be the result of a failure on the part of preachers to hold together the two themes of their message: "Jesus Christ as Lord and ourselves your servants through Jesus." Jesus said, "Let your light so shine before men, that they may see your good works and give glory to your Father who is in heaven." (Matt. 5: 16.) A particular light must shine on our good works if those works are to be part of our proclamation that Jesus is Lord; but if there be no "works" what is the light to illuminate? I am not speaking in a general sense about the necessity of preachers living the Christian life, I am speaking specifically about the necessity of preachers being servants, that is, of being engaged in making the Lordship of Jesus Christ known and accepted in some area of human living.

The message that Jesus Christ is Lord is timeless truth; the life of the servant is to serve the present age. It is his business to invest his life in some task or tasks of obedience whereby not only does he fulfil his own calling, but also helps others to see what a Christian ought to believe as well as what he ought to do. A country pastor is doing just that by the way in which

59

he serves his people; Karl Barth is doing just that by the public letters he writes to his friend Josef Hromadka; Paul Devanandan is doing just that in his search for a presentation of the Christian faith which will reveal its relevance to the Indian scene. But when one thinks of a pure preacher, so called, who is not involved in any struggle to serve the world at some specific point of obedience, then one is thinking of someone whose message and teaching can provide people with a theology about their faith but not with a theological understanding of their lives. St. Paul calls such men "peddlers of God's word". (2 Cor. 2: 17.) He says he is different from them because, as he reminds the church at Corinth, he has been both their preacher and servant, and the Corinthian church was itself written on his heart. "You are my certificate yourselves," he says, "written on my heart, recognized and read by all men." (2 Cor. 3: 2, Moffatt.)

> A charge to keep I have,
>   A God to glorify,
> A never dying soul to save,
>   And fit it for the sky;
>
> To serve the present age,
>   My calling to fulfil:
> O may it all my powers engage
>   To do my Master's will!

So sang Charles Wesley. A charge to keep, a God to glorify, a soul to save, the present age to serve—that is the preacher's calling.

This understanding of the preacher's calling as servant has also, we said, increased the attempts to get closer to the servants of the world—the workers—to meet them and to serve them where they are. Two of the newest orders in the Roman Catholic Church—the little brothers of Jesus and the little sisters of Jesus— seek to make quite plain that the calling of the preacher is to be servant. These brothers and sisters learn some skill that will enable them to serve their fellow-men in some secular occupation. There are two of these little brothers in my own home town in Jaffna working regularly as masons. St. Paul too was a servant like this. He maintained his position as a worker by making tents. There can be no mistake when a preacher is also a servant in this sense. He is so obviously a servant.

The worker-priests were servants too. Their aim was to share the life of the workmen to whom they went with their message of Jesus. They were following the example of St. Paul who, though he was free from all men, made himself a slave to all that he might win the more. "To the Jews I became as a Jew," he wrote, "in order to win Jews; to those outside the law I became as one outside the law that I might win those outside the law. To the weak I became weak, that I might win the weak. I have become all things to all men, that I might by all means save some." (1 Cor. 9: 19–22.) What can be more natural, therefore, than for those who have been called to be servants to become actual servants taking their place alongside their fellows whose primary occupation is as servants in the world! The pastors who go to Iona engage in this same task of identification. Priest and workman—they work together, worship together, and seek together to understand the secular implications of the Lordship of Christ.

But this being said, it is necessary also to say something more to avoid misunderstanding. It is necessary to remember that those who have sought these methods of identification with the "workmen" of the world are not thereby intending an example which all must follow. Rather, they are seeking only to demonstrate in one particular form the meaning of the obedience to which all are called. One fact, however, must be common to the life of all servants and that is that the arrangements for their livelihood will be such as not to destroy or distort their connection with those whom they are seeking to serve. The tent-making ministry of St. Paul ensured this in one way, the basing of church-finance on congregational giving ensures this in another.

The underlying issue here is important and I cannot do better than illustrate it by using the great unsolved problem of the so-called younger churches as an example. How can we in the younger churches relate missionary-support to self-support in such a way as not to violate either the calling of the preacher to servant-hood or the essential interdependence of churches which is given to us in the one Body? There is no easy answer to this question, but some new answer must be found and found soon, for there are present practices which are making theological obedience in this area increasingly impossible. Missionaries and fraternal-workers in Japan, for instance, are inexorably separated from those among whom they have come to work by the size of the salaries which they receive: or in India, the bishops of the Methodist Church are cut loose from any essential dependence on the faithful giving of their people because bishops' salaries practically come from abroad.

The primary calling of the preacher is to be a servant: that has been the burden of this address. But before I conclude I must make one thing plain: that in speaking of "preachers" there is no intention not to speak about

Christians generally. Indeed, it is true to say that it is every Christian who is called to be a preacher, a person who is ready to give oral witness concerning the Lordship of Christ. It is also every Christian to whom the call comes to be a servant. This is necessarily so, because the burden of Christian discipleship is not to be a religious person as such, any kind of religious person, but to be a man. Says Dietrich Bonhoeffer:

> It is not some religious act which makes a Christian what he is, but participation in the suffering of God in the life of the world. This is *metanoia*. It is not in the first instance bothering about one's own needs, problems, sins, and fears, but allowing oneself to be caught up in the way of Christ, into the Messianic event, and thus fulfilling Isaiah 53.[1]

"I am partaker with you," says St. John, the writer of the book of Revelation, "in the tribulation and kingdom and patience which are in Jesus." (Rev. 1: 9, R.V.) That sums up all we have tried to say. We are called to partake in the tribulation which is in Jesus. The love of the Master for men has made us their servants, and there is no release for us from that love. He suffers for them and we suffer with Him. We participate in "the powerlessness of God" in the world. We are called also to share in the Kingdom which is in Jesus, for the message with which we are entrusted and by which we live is that Jesus Christ is Lord. Thereby we are set free from other masters, and therein we are enabled to work the works of power that belong to the Kingdom. We are called to patience too, the patience which is in Jesus, for the final vindication of the Lord we proclaim and our own role as servants must await

[1] *Letters and Papers from Prison* (Macmillan Co.), pp. 169, 166

the Lord's hour of triumph. Then "he shall see the
fruit of the travail of his soul and be satisfied".
(Is. 53: 11.)

Now the God of peace, who brought again from the dead
the great shepherd of the sheep with the blood of the
eternal covenant, even our Lord Jesus, make you perfect
in every good thing to do his will, working in us that which
is well-pleasing in his sight, through Jesus Christ; to whom
be the glory for ever and ever. Amen.

(Heb. 13: 20–21, R.V.)

3

Not every one who says to me, "Lord, Lord," shall enter the kingdom of heaven, but he who does the will of my Father who is in heaven.

On that day many will say to me, "Lord, Lord, did we not prophesy in your name, and in your name do many mighty works?"

And then I will declare to them, "I never knew you; depart from me, you evil doers."

(Matt. 7: 21–23.)

Lord of the harvest, who dost sow good seed into the hearts of all men: grant that our hearts may not be so hardened by the world's traffic that the seed can take no root; nor so shallow that the roots can find no depth; nor so cumbered that the growing shoots are choked; but that we may be good ground to the glory of Thy name. Amen.

G. W. Briggs (from *Daily Prayer*, Oxford University Press).

3. The Servant and His Master

*No longer do I call you servants, for the servant does
not know what his master is doing; but I have called
you friends. (John 15: 15.)*

AMONG the parables of Jesus a very large number are
about servants and masters, and all of them have this
peculiarity that they are concerned with the behaviour
of servants in relation to their master's own action or
activity, his presence among them or his absence from
them. What the master does, or where the master is,
is the determining fact in the parable, and the point
of the parable is always to judge the behaviour of the
servant in the light of the master's purpose.

Jesus calls these parables, stories about the Kingdom.
In every case, He begins His parables with these words:
"If you would understand the Kingdom of God then
listen to this story. That is what the Kingdom of God
is like." What is it like? It is like the relationship
between servants and their master, with their master
himself active in doing. But always there is this difference
between the servant in the parable and the servant in fact,
the difference that the servants of Jesus know what their
Master is doing. At least, they are invited to know.

Indeed, only as the servants of Jesus understand this
invitation to know what their Master is doing will they
also understand why this invitation is linked to the
command of love, the command under which they stand
as servants and which they must fulfil. "As the Father
has loved me," says Jesus, "so have I loved you; abide

67

in my love." (John 15: 9.) When the translators of the
Septuagint used the word *pais* to translate the Hebrew
ebed they were not being arbitrary. The servant in the
Isaianic servant-songs was indeed *pais*. He was a member of the Father's home, part of the Father's life, loved by
the Father, who knew what His Father was doing. And
now this *pais*, this Servant-Son, was inviting His fellow-servants to their share in the Father's love and their participation in the Father's purpose. The servants must love
one another because the Servant has loved them all.

As servants, certainly, they will have many duties to
perform, but the first obligation of their servanthood
will be to love their fellow-servants. On the exercise of
that love, which was in fact to share in the Master's
love for them all, depended what they could do for
Him. Apart from Jesus the servant could do nothing.
But there was also only one way in which the servant
could abide in Jesus, share His life and partake in His
strength, and that was to love his brethren, his fellow-servants. By the exercise of that love alone could each
servant share in the Master's love for them all. "Abide
in me," said Jesus, "for I am the vine and you are the
branches. He who abides in me and I in him, he it is
that bears much fruit. You did not choose me but I
chose you and appointed you that you go and bear
fruit and that your fruit should abide." (John 15: 5, 16.)

It is clear, is it not, that here we have a picture of
what it means to be a servant that is quite unique?
Each servant is called and engrafted into the Master's
life. That life is spent in love. And each servant abides
in the Master's love and draws strength from it as he
also shares that love of the Master for his fellow-servants. So a fellowship of servants is created as the
primary fact, a fellowship on which is wholly dependent

the ability of each servant to fulfil his duties. In fact, even this fulfilment of his duties is something which the servant asks and receives. No servant can bear fruit of himself; he must ask and receive it from the Father. It is the Father who is the vine-dresser. He planted the vine. By Him the vine and its branches are tended. And, because of Him, the branches bear fruit. It does not matter how difficult any task of any servant may be, "if you abide in me," said Jesus, "and my words abide in you—that is, if you love as I have commanded you—ask whatever you will, and it shall be done for you". (John 15: 7.) "I have appointed you that whatever you ask the Father in my name, he may give it to you." (John 15: 16.)

> We who in Christ believe
> That He for us hath died,
> We all His unknown peace receive
> And feel His blood applied.
>
> Stronger than death and hell
> The mystic power we prove;
> And conquerors of the world, we dwell
> In heaven, who dwell in love.
>
> His Spirit to us He gave,
> And dwells in us we know;
> The witness in ourselves we have,
> And all its fruits we show.[1]

It is at our peril that we minimize or forget this scriptural connection between love and service, our love for the brethren and our service to the world. Actually, we know quite well that we do not stand or serve by ourselves. We were buried with Christ in our baptism, and in Him we lost once and for all our aloneness. Now,

[1] Charles Wesley.

we are one with others in the Body of Christ, and there is no way for us to remain apart from the common life of that Body except to cease to be members of it altogether. "We know," says the epistle of St. John, "that we have passed out of death into life, because we love the brethren. He who does not love remains in death." (I John 3: 14.) And, if one is dead, how can he do the works that pertain to eternal life? We either love and live and work, or we become dead branches which must be cut down and put into the fire. (Cf. John 15: 6.)

The Christian witness is in the last analysis dependent on whether the presence of the Christ can be discerned in the midst of the fellowship. He said, "Where two or three are gathered together in my name, there am I" (Matt. 18: 20) and where this miracle is absent no Christian witness can actually take place. The early Church impressed the world by the message it proclaimed and by the service it rendered only because the world saw that this proclamation and this service arose from a fellowship which was outside the realm of human possibility. The outsider said to himself, "How these Christians love one another!" and, because he sought to understand and to enter into that love, he found Jesus.

Our main pre-occupation in these lectures is with the calling of preachers, the responsibilities of those who are ordained ministers of the Gospel. Does it need any further underlining to point out how weak and ineffective our ministry does become simply because we do not take seriously this truth, so thoroughly attested by scripture, that the spiritual strength and power which reside in any member are determined by the constancy with which that member resides in the whole body? If we do not love the brethren, even though we may preach with great distinction, we shall do as much good as a noisy gong; we may be able to teach with real knowledge of the truth but the effect of it will be nothing; we may even work miracles but we would not be able to bring wholeness to any life; we may serve, perhaps to the point of self-denial, but it will be all to no purpose. (Cf. 1 Cor. 13: 1–3.) The gifts we have are gifts within the one body of which we are members, and those gifts can be used to the glory of God only as by love we make our membership in that body effective. To quote Charles Wesley again:

> Hence may all our actions flow,
> Love the proof that Christ we know;
> Mutual love the token be,
> Lord, that we belong to Thee:
> Love, Thine image, love impart!
> Stamp it on our face and heart!
> Only love to us be given!
> Lord, we ask no other heaven.

Listen to what St. John has to say in his epistle. "That which we have seen and heard we proclaim also to you, so that you may have fellowship with us; and our fellowship is with the Father and with his Son Jesus Christ." (1 John 1: 3.) The reason for our preaching, says St. John, is the upbuilding of the fellowship, for on that upbuilding will depend how much and how effectively each member of the fellowship will fulfil his tasks in the world. "We receive from him whatever we ask, because we keep his commandments and do what pleases him. And this is his commandment, that we should believe in the name of his Son Jesus Christ and love one another." (1 John 3: 22–23.)

Listen to St. Paul. "In my preaching," he says, "I make the gospel free of charge. I preach it because

71

necessity is laid upon me. I have become all things to all men, that I might by all means save some. I do it all for the sake of the gospel, that I may share in its blessings." (1 Cor. 9: 18, 16, 22, 23.) St. Paul gets his share of the blessings of the Gospel by taking it to others. There is no other way in which he can make the Gospel-blessing his own.

Listen also to St. Peter. "Having purified your souls," he says, "by your obedience to the truth for a sincere love of the brethren, love one another earnestly from the heart. You have been born anew through the living and abiding word of God. That word is the good news which was preached to you. So put away all malice and all guile and insincerity and envy and all slander." (1 Pet. 1: 22–2: 1.) The Gospel that was preached, says St. Peter, was the good news that being born anew you would have the capacity to love. Let that, then, be your first concern, for on it everything else depends.

The love of the brethren, the preaching of the Gospel, one's own share in the Gospel's blessing: all three belong together as one circle of truth each dependent on and each productive of the other two. And from this circle of truth no preacher may seek to escape. The true status of the preacher is that he is servant, the real secret of the servant is that he is friend. He is called to work with his Master and not just for Him. He is engaged with other servants with whom he must work. And all the servants together are invited to share in the counsels of the whole enterprise, to draw from the strength of their Master's own service and each to find sustenance for his own ministry from the friendship of his fellows. "This is my commandment," are the words of Jesus, "that you love one another as I have loved you." (John 15: 12.)

All this said, let us now turn to a closer consideration of the servant-parables of Jesus as we find them in the gospels. Some of these parables were addressed to His disciples, some to the crowd in general, and some to the religious leaders of the day, but in all of them there is set out for us a picture of what it is that the Master expects from His servants, and what kind of servants we must be if we are to share in the work and the purposes of the Master.

First of all, there is the situation in which the master has gone on a long journey. His return will not be for a considerable time. And, in the meanwhile, his servants have been left with the responsibility of carrying on the master's business. Each servant does his share with what has been committed to him. The man with five talents makes five more, and the man with two talents makes two more. There is no rivalry between them, or jealousy, because the master has adjudged them not equal in ability and, therefore, has given to one of them five talents while to the other he has given only two. In fact, it is evident that this distinction between them makes no difference to the equality of their calling. As, in the story of the pounds, each servant receives the same amount, each is servant equally with the rest.

Then the master comes back and summons his servants to render an account of their stewardship. The servants who have done well are commended. Their rewards are different, but to each the same commendation is given. He who has made ten pounds is made governor over ten cities, while he who has made five pounds is made governor over five cities. Then comes the servant who has done nothing. He has been afraid lest he should lose or spoil that which was committed to him. Suppose he should make some mistake which

73

would bring discredit to the master! Suppose he should not do as well as the master would expect of him! He comes to the master and says to him, "Here is what is yours. I have kept it safe." But that is the one thing that the servant should not have worried about. The safety of the master's business is the master's business. The servant is simply set to work and no excuse is good enough for not working.

It is not only fear, though, and indolence which have been the problem; there has also been the reluctance to work for a master who will himself take all the profit. What shall I get out of it? the servant says to himself. Precisely nothing, for I am only a slave. Why, then, must I worry? My master reaps where he has not sown—why must I sow for him? My master takes up what he does not lay down—why must I invest for him? The servant has forgotten that a master who is so closely intent on the progress of his business will also not overlook such a waste of time and opportunity on the part of his servant. "Take from him that which he has and give it to the first servant." Certainly it means additional work for the first servant, but where one servant is slack another has to bear the burden. Only, with more work there is given more grace also. As for the servant who has done nothing, "Cast him out—he is useless." (Matt. 25: 14–30; Lk. 19: 12–27.)

In the parable about the master who leased his vineyard, the situation is radically different from that in the parable of the talents or of the pounds. In this story, the master has gone away but the servants are not left alone. The master constantly sends them messengers to remind them that the vineyard is not theirs and that lease-rent is due to him. They must make regular acknowledgment that the vineyard is his. But the servants want to appropriate the vineyard and so refuse to pay any lease-rent. And, when the son comes, they say to themselves, "The owner must be dead, that is why the son is coming. Let us kill the son and the vineyard will be ours." For the law provided that the estate of a proselyte who died intestate should be regarded as ownerless property belonging to whomsoever was already in occupation. But can the vineyard be thus expropriated? The servants soon find out that it cannot be. It is they who are finally put out of the vineyard. The master's property is always his. How easily we who serve Him in the Church forget this! How often we tend to act as if God's truth was our tradition, God's light was our enlightenment, God's gifts were our heritage! And, how violently we seek to defend these things which we have made ours! God must have free access to His own vineyard, and where any present tenant attempts to prevent Him, the warning of Jesus is plain that the tenant will be removed. (Matt. 21: 33–42.)

In the parable of the wheat and the tares, it is another aspect of the same truth about the master's ownership which is taught. The servants sow at the master's bidding, but when tares also come up the servants want to pull out these tares. The master, however, bids them wait till harvest time. Their decision as to what is wheat and which are tares can be quite premature and wrong. The master will not allow even one wheat stalk to be pulled out by mistake. The servants must learn to wait till the master himself pronounces judgment. Until then! Until then the servants must not act as if the field was theirs and they could do as they were able. (Matt. 13: 24–30.)

But, while this teaching about respecting God's

75

ownership is quite plain, there is also the invitation given to men to invest everything they have in acquiring possession of that which is God's. The mistake in the man who buried the talent was that he felt unable to use that talent as if it was his. He was overawed by the fact that it belonged to the master. He was afraid that he would lose it or spoil it. Jesus says to His servants, "You must learn to act like that man who was ploughing in his master's field; who, when his plough struck against a buried treasure, went and sold everything that he had and bought that field." (Matt. 13: 44.) We cannot work for God unless we make His work our work by putting everything we have into it. We can do this at no less a price. The steward who was suddenly called upon to submit his accounts acted with great presence of mind and resourcefulness. (Lk. 16: 1–13.) With how little care and concern we act when faced with some crisis of decision in the course of our work for God! That work has not sufficiently become our work. Our everything does not depend on what happens to it. All we have and all we are have not been invested in it. Therefore, we are content to let things take their own course. As Jesus makes the master say in the parable of the dishonest steward, "The sons of this world are wiser in their own generation than the sons of light."

A third situation depicted in the parables of Jesus about masters and servants is that in which the master has gone away but his return is imminent. No one knows whether he will come at midnight or at dawn. Therefore the servants who have been asked to make ready and to watch for his coming are tempted to make the most of his absence. There is the servant who drinks and gets drunk and ill-treats his fellow-servants. (Lk. 12: 45.) There is the servant who goes to sleep saying the master will not come now. (Mk. 13: 36.) But there are also the servants who keep awake (Lk. 12: 37) and, when their master comes, are able to report that every duty which was set has been accomplished (v. 43). It is true that when the master comes he will not say to his faithful servants, "You can rest now because your work is done and you have done well." No master acts like that. He will say rather, "Come and wait on me, I must have my supper." (Lk. 17: 7–10.) We are unprofitable servants whatever be our achievement. There is never anything owing to us.

A slave does not change his status by being a good slave. A servant does not change his status by being set in authority over his fellow-servants. The status of the servant always remains unchanged. Some of the parables of Jesus deal with this truth and emphasize it. They teach us that the status of the servant is fundamentally a status in relation to his master and to no one else. The labourers who came to work in the vineyard discovered that when pay-time came. Those who had come first demanded justice, but they soon saw that their demand for justice was in reality a demand for them to be treated as relative to their fellows. As far as the master was concerned, it was his grace that had hired them all and given them work to do; it was also his grace which paid each one of them as the master himself thought right. Each servant stood in direct relation to the master. Their relative position to each other was quite irrelevant. (Matt. 20: 1–16.)

In the parable of the two servants this truth is given further significance. One servant had lent some money to the other, but he himself had borrowed a large sum from his master. The master forgave him his debt, but he would not forgive his debtor. Then he discovered that his unforgivingness lost him his own forgiveness. For the second servant was not simply a debtor to the first, he too was actually a debtor to the master. It was out of the master's loan that the first servant had lent to the second. Apart from the master's bounty the first servant would not have had anything to lend. The master's forgiveness, therefore, included both servants; so that the first in refusing to forgive the second was actually refusing to allow that the master should forgive. To refuse to forgive is to refuse to be forgiven. (Matt. 18: 23–35.) In every way we need to beware lest we assume that we can lord it over somebody else. Each servant is servant of the master and retains that status.

Finally, there is the situation in which the work of the servant is part of the total activity of the master himself, and is determined by it. The servants going in search of guests for the man who was giving a banquet (Lk. 14: 16f.), the innkeeper receiving the wounded man whom the Samaritan brings to the door (Lk. 10: 30f.), the shepherd entering the sheepfold to take the sheep out to pasture (John 10: 9, 2)—all have their obedience determined by what the master has done and is doing. The master has prepared the feast, the master has found a wounded man by the roadside, the master sits in the doorway of his sheepfold. "Working together with him"—that was St. Paul's phrase to describe the servant's role. (2 Cor. 6: 1.) He works, and we who are members of His Body find ourselves inevitably involved in His ministry.

I do not believe that it is mere accident that Jesus has given us so many parables about masters and servants. I believe that the figure of the servant was never far away from His mind; and that in teaching His disciples about the Kingdom, He saw the necessity of impressing upon them the truth that they could not inherit the blessings of the Kingdom except as servants of the King. He knew Himself to be the Servant, the one in whom the scripture about the Servant was fulfilled (Lk. 4: 21), and He saw His disciples as following in His footsteps. "It is enough," He often said to His disciples, "that the servant be as his lord." Indeed, it was clear to Jesus that even if His servants distantly approximated to what His servants should be, if only in some measure they could be the kind of servants which, through His parables, He had taught them to be; then they would inevitably have also to walk along the road He walked—a road which, starting from the humility and humiliation of Bethlehem, wound its way in blessing through the little towns and villages of Palestine until it led to the loneliness of Gethsemane and the sacrifice of Calvary. And then, going past, disappeared through an empty tomb, becoming for ever a way without an ending.

> A disciple is not above his teacher, nor a servant above his master; it is enough for the disciple to be like his teacher, and the servant like his master. If they have called the master of the house Beelzebul, how much more will they malign those of his household. You are not of the world, but I chose you out of the world, therefore the world hates you. It has hated me before it hated you. Remember the word that I said to you, A servant is not greater than his master.
>
> (Matt. 10: 24–25; John 15: 18–20.)

Just twenty-five years ago, in 1933, I had completed my theological studies at the United Theological College in Bangalore. I was filled up to the ears with information about the kinds of things we study in a theological college, but as a preacher of the Gospel I was still fumbling. That year we were visited at the college by the Burma Gospel Team, and my principal asked me to join them and go with them to their next mission in Hyderabad. Somehow my experience with the team scared me. Its work was largely modelled on the teachings of what at that time was called the Oxford Group, with the result that I found that whenever I had to speak at their meetings I had to speak about myself. It was true that I spoke about my Lord, and yet it was always about how wonderful my Lord had been to me. How was I to witness to Him in such a way as to help people to think of Him and Him only? In the December of that year I went to Allahabad to attend the Quadrennial Conference of the Student Christian Movement of India, Burma and Ceylon, and there I heard for the first time Dr. Visser 't Hooft speak. He spoke on the Lordship of Christ, a truth I had always known, but somehow he made me see that this Lordship was more than a message to be proclaimed. It required of the messenger a particular relationship both to his Lord as well as to his hearers. For twenty-five years I have sought by study and discipleship (such discipleship as the Lord has given to me in spite of my sins, and through friendship and converse with fellow-Christians in many lands) to understand the nature of this relationship, until now I feel some confidence in speaking about it.

John the Baptist spoke of himself as a voice. (John 1: 23.) He was the sound proceeding from the lips of someone else. Someone else was speaking, not speaking through John, but speaking; and John himself was the word spoken. He was the voice, the sound, the message of the speaker. The servant stands in such a relationship to his Master that two things take place simultaneously. The servant bears witness to his Master, and the Master bears witness to His servant. The question is not simply that of John witnessing about God but also of God witnessing about John. God calls His witnesses and makes it clear to the world that they are His witnesses, so clear that the witnesses are able to say, God has spoken and we are the voice. When God establishes someone as the servant of Jesus Christ, that in itself is God's witness that Jesus Christ is Lord; so that when the servant proclaims Christ's Lordship, he is able to attest that proclamation by his own servanthood.

This way by which God constitutes His witnesses by constituting them servants, and then by witnessing to them, was clearly explained by Jesus Himself. "I can do nothing on my own authority," He said. "I am servant. I seek not my own will but the will of him who sent me. And yet, if I bear witness to myself, my testimony is not true; there is another who bears witness to me. For the works which the Father has granted me to accomplish, these very works which I am doing, bear me witness that the Father has sent me. And the Father who sent me has himself borne witness to me." (John 5: 30–37.)

In our first lecture we have already called attention to the importance of remembering that it is Jesus who is the giver and the preacher who is the gift. He sends us: so that if there is any truth in the statement that we take Him, that truth is dependent exclusively on the fact that He does not send us alone. He comes with us to work through us those works of power which are His witness that we are His witnesses. "My speech and my message," wrote St. Paul to the Corinthians, "were not in plausible words of wisdom, but in demonstration of the Spirit. For the kingdom of God does not consist in talk but in power." (1 Cor. 2: 4; 4: 20.) Speaking to his fellow-Christians St. Peter wrote, "Once you were no people but now you are God's people, that you may declare the wonderful deeds of him who called you out of darkness into his marvellous light." (1 Pet. 2: 10, 9.) His deeds are declared by His people, His mighty acts of the past attested by His mighty acts through them in the present. In the words of St. Athanasius, "It is he himself who brought death to nought who daily raises monuments to his victory in his own disciples."

"I have called you friends"—that was the text with which we began, and we can see now how it expresses all that needs to be said about our discipleship. He is our Master and we are His servants: and our witness to Him is sustained by His witness to us; our surrender to Him is made possible by His own surrender to us.

> Lord, my time is in Thy hand,
>   My soul to Thee convert;
> Thou canst make me understand,
>   Though I am slow of heart;
> Thine in whom I live and move,
>   Thine the work, the praise is Thine;
> Thou art wisdom, power, and love,
>   And all Thou art IS MINE.[1]

So we come to the conclusion of our argument, a conclusion which can be summarized in this way. The Church is called to witness; that is why there are preachers. Preachers are called to be servants; that is why the Church exists in the world as a servant-community. The servants are bound together in a common love which is the basis of the Church's fellowship. The *koinonia* is the *koinonia* of those engaged in *diakonia*, the *diakonia* is the *diakonia* of those engaged

[1] Charles Wesley.

in *marturia*, the *marturia* is the *marturia* of the *koinonia*. All three—*marturia*, *diakonia*, *koinonia*: witness, service, fellowship—belong together in one reality of existence, and where any one of them is missing or defective, the other two will be missing or defective also.

For example, let us think of a congregation which does not engage in *diakonia*. We shall find that the fellowship in that congregation is the fellowship of a club, the fellowship of mutual friends, the fellowship of common interests; but it will not be the *koinonia* of the Holy Spirit. And its proclamation of the Lordship of Christ will lack convincing power. It will neither challenge nor disturb anyone. On the other hand, let there be a congregation which does not put at the centre of its message the fact that Jesus Christ is Lord, and we shall find that while it may engage in various forms of service to the world it will be unable to support that service with servanthood; and that its fellowship will lack the quality of being sustained by the Master's love. Or, let there be a congregation which is careless of maintaining its fellowship, and we shall find that it soon ceases to be a community engaged in meaningful service, in service that bears testimony to Jesus as Lord. As for its witness, it will simply be a witness of words which the Lord could not acknowledge as witness to Himself. The truth must be quite clear that when we speak of the Church's call to witness, its challenge to service and its constitution as a fellowship, we are speaking not about three sets of activities in which Christians must engage but rather of an inclusive reality of which God is the author, the sustainer, and the perfecter.

That is why the New Testament, in describing the life of the Church, speaks of it as characterized not only by *marturia*, *diakonia* and *koinonia* but also by *leitourgia*.

Leitourgia is service rendered to a king. When St. Paul speaks of the rulers in the state as God's *leitourgoi*, he is testifying to God as the ruler of all. (Rom. 13: 6.) The Church is a holy nation whose life is lived in the King's service. This liturgy is rendered when by witness, fellowship and servanthood the King is glorified. *Leitourgia* is these three in their doxology. Writing to the Romans, St. Paul describes himself as a minister of Christ Jesus in the priestly service of the Gospel of God. (Rom. 15: 16.) All service is priestly when it is service of this Gospel, service to be offered to God "consecrated by the Holy Spirit". And God's holy action determines in every way the forms that this service will take. To use a phrase of St. Paul, not only will such service achieve its immediate intention, but it will also overflow in many thanksgivings to God. (2 Cor. 9: 12.)

The preacher preaches because God has declared that Jesus Christ is Lord and has given to Him a name above every name, that at the name of Jesus every knee should bow. (Phil. 2: 9–10.) The servant serves because God has loved the world and given His only Son that whosoever believes may not perish but may have life. (John 3: 16.) The fellowship happens because Jesus loves His friends and in His love, by the power of the Holy Spirit, they find that they can love one another. (John 15: 12–17.) Glory is rendered because God has shone in our hearts to give the light of the knowledge of the glory of God in the face of Christ. (2 Cor. 4: 6.) To this fourfold reality belongs the task of the servant, and apart from this it will be a quite impossible one. The life of the Church is the enduring ground of the servant's vocation.

How otherwise could he teach men those things which they must observe! How otherwise would he continue in a ministry in which, having to change many things, he would be accused of disturbing the world! How otherwise could he persist in loving and serving the poor even though they might suspect or reject him! How otherwise would he serve simply because he was servant and continue to serve until his service was over! No one could be a servant except God make him and keep him, but when God does, then is he enabled under the test of that service to glorify God by his obedience in acknowledging the Gospel. (2 Cor. 9: 13.)

What, then, is the content of this service? The content is defined by the command under which it is performed: "Love thy neighbour as thyself." (Lk. 10: 27.) There are two persons in whom God meets men— Jesus Christ and one's neighbour. And both challenge us to service. Jesus Christ demands that we accept Him as Master and serve Him; our neighbour becomes the person whom we must serve. This is because Jesus is involved in both situations. He is my Master and my Neighbour too. "I was hungry, I was thirsty, I was naked, I was in prison, I was a stranger." (Matt. 25: 31f.)—It is Jesus Christ who is speaking, but it is my neighbour He is describing. Both are one. This does not exhaust, however, the implication of the command to love—for not only do I meet Jesus Christ in my neighbour but my neighbour meets Jesus Christ in me. I am the arm of the Church stretched out to my neighbour with the love with which Christ has loved him. In other words, I must serve my neighbour as if he was Jesus Christ; I must also serve him as if I was Jesus Christ. In a real sense, the *diakonia* of the Church is the service of Jesus Christ to Jesus Christ, or to put it differently it is the Church's participation in the life of Jesus Christ in the world.

85

First of all, therefore, the content of *diakonia* will be personal charity—practical kindness to those in need. It is in the exercise of this charity that one learns the real discipline of love, for charity has to be exercised among persons as persons, and often one by one. It is easier to give a subscription to a hospital than to stop, on one's way to tennis, and pick up a drunk who has fallen into the drain and hurt himself, and deliver him at the hospital. I found it easier, writing this address, to write it than to get up from my table and deal patiently with a beggar who came to my window. "The poor have the gospel preached to them," said Jesus. (Matt. 11: 5.) It certainly was preached; for how Jesus loved them! The leper was touched and healed; the paralytic was forgiven and made to walk; the woman with the issue of blood was called out and recognized; the prostitute was allowed to touch him, even to kiss his feet. They were persons, He was charity.

The public ministry of Jesus occupied only three years, but short as this time was He always found time for persons. Our problem is that being always pressed for time, we have lost the art of charity. We are constantly hurrying, from one meeting to another, from one person to another, from one job to another; and because we are in a hurry we hardly come to grips with our surroundings. Like a tyre slipping in the mud, there is a frantic going round but no forward movement. An old missionary friend of mine, the Rev. Middleton Weaver, said to me, "When I first came to Ceylon we travelled in bullock carts, now we travel in motor-cars, and the substitution of the one for the other has even ruined our evangelistic work. Now I rush down to a meeting and then get back home; when I used to travel in a bullock cart I really met people." Yes, hurry means that we gather impressions but have no experiences, that we collect acquaintances but make no friends, that we attend meetings but experience no encounter. We must recover eternity if we are to find time, and eternity is what Jesus came to restore. For without it, there can be no charity.

But while personal charity must be the spirit of all *diakonia*, *diakonia* itself demands that the help which is given should seek to provide permanent relief. The widow, the orphan, the stranger, the displaced person, the slave—these are the people whom the prophetic movement in Judaism identified as those in particular need of *diakonia*. They were the socially defenceless. They needed to be protected against the unpredictability of the rich and the powerful. What was needed was not merely acts of personal kindness; it was necessary that the people of God should proclaim their solidarity with these people and stand between them and the sources from which their existence was being threatened. As an example of what this means, the life of Mahatma Gandhi is a striking one. A member of the wealthy and English-educated class in India, he so identified himself with his people that he became the means of their resistance to Imperial power. A member of the high-caste community, he so identified himself with the out-caste that he became their bulwark against oppression. A member of the Hindu faith, he so identified himself with the cause of the Muslims that those who preached hate against the Muslims felt compelled to murder him.

The point is this, that it is not enough for the Church to build orphanages or old-age homes; it is necessary that these institutions of the Church's *diakonia* reflect the Church's permanent concern for all who are weak and defenceless. Where that concern is absent, acts of *diakonia* are only plucked fruit. When, in Ceylon, we put up a *pandal* to accommodate the guests who have been invited to a wedding, we often plant at the entrance to the *pandal* some bamboo on either side: and on the bamboo branches there are hung bunches of coconuts. The coconuts are plucked fruit; they are not the fruit of the bamboo, they are simply part of the decoration. How often the institutions of the Church's *diakonia* are plucked fruit, hung up as part of its decoration; they are not fruit from the tree itself! It is not only the tree which must be judged by its fruit, the fruit also must be judged by the tree.

The content of Christian *diakonia* is personal charity and permanent concern, but to these two must be added a third element—social passion. Where it is clearly seen that *diakonia* is not something to be construed as an instrument of evangelism but that it possesses its own validity, then it will also be clearly seen that *diakonia* cannot stop short of the attempt to work for a re-ordering of society. When, in Ceylon, I have converted a tenant-farmer in a village, educated him and his children, so that he becomes a teacher in a school and his son becomes a lawyer, all I have done is to pull a family out of the world and bring them safely ashore into the bourgeois security of the Church there. Is it not necessary for true *diakonia* that somehow the Church must get so involved in the insecurities of society, that no one will find social security simply by joining the Church? Will not the Church only then be in a position to break up and re-new the world? It is easy to say "blessed are the poor" when we are talking to the rich; it is not so easy to say "blessed are the poor" to the poor themselves. It is an integral part of

88

the Church's *diakonia* to preach the good news to the poor.

Some of you may have heard Canon Southcott speaking last year during the Kirk-Week in Aberdeen. I read parts of his speech in Ceylon as reported in the bulletin of the British Council of Churches.[1] I would like to quote a paragraph from that speech.

> The parable of the hundred sheep [he said] ought to be retold to-day. Now there are ninety-nine out in the wilderness and only one in the fold. The Church spent most of its time mollycoddling that one and neglecting the other ninety-nine. If they thought at all about mission they thought in terms of pew-fodder. There was a vast no-man's land between the church buildings and the world outside. Our God is too small and our church buildings are too large. The task of the Church is to learn to stoop down.

To use a phrase of Dr. Hoekendijk, what the world is waiting to see is "a pantomime of salvation"[2]—living works even though without an accompanying spoken text.

> Draw in the latchstring, lad, and close the door,
> Lest those who faint without from toil and pain
> Shall rob thee of thine own too meagre store.
> Such is the world's advice.
> But—there was One who flung it open wide—
> And He was crucified.

Now to him that is able to stablish you according to . . . the preaching of Jesus Christ, according to the revelation of the mystery . . . made known unto all the nations unto obedience of faith, to the only wise God, through Jesus Christ, be the glory for ever. Amen. (Rom. 16: 25–27, R.V.)

[1] No. 72, p. 12.   [2] Article in *Wending*, Jan. 1957.

4

Therefore, holy brethren, who share in a heavenly call, consider Jesus, the apostle and high priest of our confession. He was faithful to him who appointed him, just as Moses also was faithful in God's house.

Now Moses was faithful in all God's house as a servant, but Christ was faithful over God's house as a son.

And we are his house if we hold fast our confidence and pride in our hope. For we share in Christ.

(Heb. 3: 1–6, 14.)

O Lord God, when Thou givest to Thy servants to endeavour any great matter, grant us also to know that it is not the beginning, but the continuing of the same unto the end, until it be thoroughly finished, which yieldeth the true glory; through Him who for the finishing of Thy work laid down His life, our redeemer, Jesus Christ. Amen.

Attributed to Sir Francis Drake.

4. The Servant in His Master's Prayer

He is able for all time to save those who draw near to God through him, since he always lives to make intercession for them. (Heb. 7: 25.)

ABOUT forty years ago a man came to a little Hindu temple at Palani, a small village in South India, bringing a cock to be sacrificed. By the time he arrived at the top of the hill where the temple was it was late in the evening and the temple doors were closed. So he came down to the bottom of the hill and waited in the village till the next morning. While he was waiting, he heard somebody singing nearby. He went to see who it was. Someone gave him a little book about a man called Jesus, and he went back for the night to read that little book to while away his time.

The next morning he sacrificed his cock and went home. Within a few days he was on the road looking for the person who gave him that book. He wanted to be a follower of Jesus. He walked many miles to come to Dindigul where Mr. Elwood lived who had preached that evening at Palani. He told him of his quest, only to receive the reply that his home did not come within the area of operation of Mr. Elwood's church. This was a place where the American Congregationalists were working, whereas the man's home was far away, and was probably in the area where the London Mission was at work. So he trudged several miles to go to

Erode to Mr. Popley, only to be told again that the right person to go to was Mr. Ellis, the British Methodist missionary in Dharapuram. There he went finally, and there he was baptized. To-day, out of that particular beginning, have come forty thousand Christians.[1]

"Jesus Christ is able for all time since he always lives. He is able since he always lives to make intercession." Every story of the Church's triumph is like this story, a story of guided accident, of human weakness and of disproportionate result. The story of the Church is always the story of God as He builds it.

Throughout these lectures our emphasis has been on the continuing work of Christ, and in this lecture it will be on one aspect of that work, His continuing intercession for those who draw near to God through Him. The most powerful force in the world is and has always been the praying ministry of the Ascended Christ, which it is well for us to remember as we ponder over the calling and the work of preachers. Nothing which preachers do can have either substance or result apart from this ministry of their Lord. He prays for them, He prays for those whom they seek to shepherd in His name, He prays for those whom they seek to bring into His fold, He prays for Himself as the Great Shepherd of all.

In the seventeenth chapter of St. John's gospel is our Lord's great prayer of intercession, and it is on this prayer that we shall meditate, seeking to make it our own. We need to make it our own, not only by placing ourselves within it and accepting gladly that it shall be for us, but also by learning to pray ourselves as Jesus prayed for those to whom in His name we seek to

[1] Story told by Bishop Lesslie Newbigin and here retold from memory.

92

minister. His prayer for them must become our prayer for them also.

The calling of a preacher is the calling to be servant. We have seen how this is so and what it involves. But we shall not have learnt the inner meaning of our servanthood until we have learned from our Lord that our greatest service is rendered through the ministry of prayer. Our Lord said to Peter, "I have prayed for you." (Lk. 22: 32.) That prayer guarded Peter through the hours of darkness and temptation, led him out from the place of his denial into bitter repentance, and finally brought him face to face with his risen Lord. When the preacher has preached, and the servant has served, there still remains to be done the one thing which alone can take all that has been done and said, and make them available for the Master's use. We need to pray—pray for ourselves who are His witnesses, pray for our hearers who are His children, and for all those whom we seek to serve who are His brethren. It is in the ministry of prayer that we enter most directly into the ministry of the Christ. He prays and we pray with Him, the Holy Spirit praying within us teaching us how to pray. (Rom. 8: 26–27.)

But the importance of this is not simply that by prayer we bring to God and place at His disposal all that we have done and attempted in His name; but that also prayer teaches us what to do. He is blessed who has learnt to make his prayer-life control his actions and his words. Our normal method of obedience is to pray for God's guidance and help in the things that we have to do, then to do them, and then to pray for God's forgiveness for the things we have done wrong and for His over-ruling blessing on all that we have sought to do for Him. This is right as far as it goes, but there is another dimension, is there not, to the prayer-life! There is such a meeting with God as will decide what we shall do, and decide it in advance.

I was told a story about something that happened when Sadhu Sundar Singh came to Great Britain which illustrates vividly what I have in mind. The story may have apocryphal elements in it, but anyone who knows the two people concerned in the story will accept it as in character. When Sadhu Sundar Singh was to come to Great Britain, his programme was put into the hands of William Paton, the late General Secretary of the International Missionary Council. It seems Dr. Paton arranged his programme and sent a copy of it to the Sadhu. The Sadhu replied, "I want three hours every morning set apart for prayer, from 4.30 to 7.30, and I shall tell you what the Holy Spirit says to me when I pray." Dr. Paton was a little taken aback by this reply, but there was nothing else to do except to write to the various people in charge of the Sadhu's pro-gramme in the various centres and tell them what the position was. The Sadhu had a tremendously blessed time in this country, and when his work was over and he was leaving for India, Dr. Paton and many other friends went to see him off at Tilbury. As the ship sailed, and as the good-byes were waved, it seems Dr. Paton pulled out his handkerchief and wiped his brow and said, "This is the last time that I shall undertake to arrange a programme for anyone under the direct guidance of the Holy Spirit. It is too exhausting."

Who will teach us to pray, and how shall we learn?

That great missionary man of prayer, Fraser of Lisuland, once wrote, "I feel the need of trusting Him to lead me in prayer as well as in other matters. We must get our prayers from God." We must. But how shall we? Our attempt will be to answer this question, by seeking so to enter into the prayer of our Lord that we shall find it to be a prayer for us; and finding it so, experience it also as the basis of our prayer for others.

"*I have overcome the world*"—that is the point at which the prayer begins. The powers of evil have been dethroned, the prince of this world has been cast out (John 12: 31), the world Jesus loved has been conquered and redeemed, the persons for whom He prays are already His. We often forget, when we intercede for others, that we too are able to do this only because Jesus has overcome the world and because those for whom we pray are already remembered in His prayer of intercession. Our prayers both for ourselves and for our fellows need to have that quiet strength that belongs to prayers already granted. That is our victory, even our faith. (1 John 5: 4.)

Speaking to the children of Israel, as they stood on the bank of the Red Sea, with the waters in front and Pharaoh's army behind, Moses said to them, "Fear not, stand firm, and see the salvation of the Lord, which he will work for you to-day; for the Egyptians whom you see to-day, you shall never see again. The Lord will fight for you, and you have only to be still." (Ex. 14: 13–14.) That is what it means for us to enter into the prayer of Jesus and appropriate it for ourselves. He engages the enemy; we inherit His victory. He overcomes the Egyptians; we shall never see the Egyptians again. He fights for us; we have only to be still.

Jesus prays to His Father. His prayer begins with that one word of address. He lived so intensely and intimately in His Father's presence, that He was able in a moment to call Him, to turn in a moment to Him . *Jesus lifted up his eyes to heaven and said, "Father."* That

95

is how the evangelist records it. He goes from earth to heaven because He is in heaven all the time. The psalmist has said, "Blessed are the men in whose heart are the highways to Zion." (Ps. 84: 5.) Indeed, how blessed! What wonderful power there is in the lives of those who have trodden unceasingly and regularly the road to Zion, until that road has become for them a highway. Now they are able to run along that road with unerring feet, and arrive at the presence of the Father in the twinkling of an eye. The essential task to which we are committed as preachers can be performed only as we take those whom we serve into the Father's presence. But how shall we take them there unless we know the way?

"*Father*," says Jesus, "*the hour has come.*" The hour for what? For the Father's glory to be made manifest in the Son, for the Son to receive the splendour of God's love as it is poured out. The Greeks have come and gone, and Jesus has refused to go with them. (John 12: 20–21, 36b.) He has chosen to stay with the work that the Father has committed to Him. Now, the hour has come for that outpouring of love by which alone His witness to the Father can be sealed. And He is ready. "It is necessary," He says, "that the Son of man should suffer." (Cf. Mk. 8: 31.) We who are pastors know what this means. We too have seen the hour arrive, the hour when only patient poured-out love makes sense; and when, because it is done, we too receive God's witness to us that He loves us. The basic fact on which everything depends is not whether I love God but whether He loves me; not whether I believe in God but whether He believes in me. And I know the answer to these questions, and know it every time that God makes me the instrument of His loving.

Upon the sandy shore an empty shell,
Beyond the shell infinity of sea;
O Saviour, I am like that empty shell,
Thou art the Sea to me.

A sweeping wave rides up the shore, and lo,
Each dim recess the coilèd shell within
Is searched, is filled, is filled to overflow
By water crystalline.

Not to the shell is any glory then:
All glory give we to the glorious sea.
And not to me is any glory when
Thou overflowest me.[1]

"*Father, glorify thy Son that the Son may glorify thee.*"
That is where we begin. We begin with a prayer for
ourselves who pray for others. We must learn what it is
to be loved and to live as those who are loved, before
we can love. The crucial problem in Christian service
lies not at the point where service is rendered but at the
point where that service is received. No man wants to
be served. Any man resents being put under a sense of
obligation to someone else. So that, if service is to be
truly rendered and received, it must be made quite
obvious that he who serves, serves only because he has
already received; and that which he gives he gives not
out of his own bounty but out of the bounty of Him
from whom all gifts proceed. The Father loves the Son,
making it possible for the Son to love us; the Son loves
us, making it possible for us to love one another.

"*Father, Thou hast given the Son power to give eternal
life,*" says Jesus. In that power is His glory. And yet
He prays that men may receive this eternal life. Why

[1] Amy Carmichael, *Toward Jerusalem* (S.P.C.K. and the
Dohnavur Fellowship), p. 68.

does He pray? Can He not just give it? No: for eternal life is to know the only true God and Jesus Christ whom He has sent. Men must know, and it is because men must know that the Father's glory in the Son must be seen. Also, just as men must know the Father and Jesus Christ whom the Father has sent, so they must know Jesus Christ and us who are His messengers. Christian witness happens not simply when the witness is heard but when the witness himself is recognized.

There are many people who are adepts at discovering excuses for their lack of faith or obedience. They often claim that they have been caused to stumble by someone who they thought was a good Christian. My invariable answer to such people is to ask them why, when they had seen a stone on the road, they had, as it were, run at it, and so fallen over it. There is no necessity to stumble over stumbling-blocks. Jesus certainly spoke about stones of stumbling and little ones who stumble over them. (Matt. 18: 6–7.) Very few of those who boast that they have stumbled belong, however, to this category of little ones. But because there are little ones, woe unto him who is an occasion of stumbling. The concern that a witness to Jesus must be recognizable is, therefore, a necessary concern. For where that is not so, little ones will stumble and the rest will use it as an excuse. But how does such recognition come? In our own experience with those who have helped us most to get closer to Jesus, we know that it comes by the quality of their very presence. They carry conviction because there is always about them the sweet smell of that other land where they habitually dwell.

It is essential, then, that not only should my witness to my Lord be heard, but that His witness to me should be seen. *I glorified thee on earth*, prayed Jesus, *and now*,

Father, glorify thou me. The Son is praying for the Father's witness to Him, in order that He may be recognized as having been sent by the Father. Knowledge of the Father and of the Son is eternal life, so that this recognition of the Son as having been sent by the Father is of central importance. Equally important will be the recognition also of all those whom the Son will send as His witnesses.

It is within the fellowship of God's people, those who are sent by the Father and the Son in the power of the Holy Spirit, that there comes and grows that knowledge which is eternal life. How fundamental, then, it is for the fellowship that not only should the good news of the Gospel be rightly apprehended but also that its messengers should be seen in relation to it. It is part of the good news that the good news is announced and that God arranges for this, as it is part of the prayer which every witness prays that he should be known for what he is, a witness sent by Jesus Christ. Somehow, as the tools of a pastor's job increase in number and effectiveness, there is the temptation to forget what the goal of a pastor's job is. There is psychotherapy for the mentally ill, there are medicine and surgery for the physically ill, there is community reconstruction for the socially deprived : but Lord, I pray that they may know Thee, and me whom Thou has sent.

In the prayer of Jesus, there follows at this point a prayer specifically for His disciples. " *Thou gavest them to me,*" He says to the Father. "*Now, they know Me. I have given them Thy word. I am glorified in them.*" How every Christian, about whom the Master prays in this fashion, longs for the time when he himself can say this prayer with respect to someone else whose care has been his concern! What will we not give in order that we may be able to say, "Father, Thou gavest him to me. Now he knows me. I have given him Thy word. I am glorified in him"? Jesus said to His disciples, "You are they who have been with me, who have stood by me in all my temptations." (Cf. Lk. 22: 28.) He had himself lived by the love and companionship of those He had come to save. He served them best by allowing them to serve Him. He was found among them in weakness and they rejoiced in being able to love Him and minister to Him. He was glorified in them. We, most of us, have not yet learnt how to serve God or man in weakness. We do not know the secret of being God's servants to others by opening ourselves to receive their service. For us too there is no glory except as we are glorified in them.

So Jesus prays for us: "*Holy Father, keep them in thy name which thou hast given me.*" There is no other way in which God can watch over us except by keeping us true to the name which we bear, and which we have received from Jesus Christ. African Christians in the Mau Mau country, writing to their fellow-Christians outside, asked simply for one thing. "Pray for us," they said, "not that we may be kept safe but that we may be kept faithful." There is no other safety that a Christian can desire except the safety of his faith, his faith to live and die as a witness of the Name. And where this faith is present, there is present also the power to maintain the unity of that Name. "Holy Father," Jesus said, "keep them in thy name which thou hast given me, *that they may be one, even as we are one.*"

Obedience to the call to be faithful in mission is also the condition of obedience to the call to remain in unity, and both belong together in the one life. This life comes to birth through the Word. "I have given them thy word," says Jesus; "*Thy word is truth.*" When God speaks, He calls by name, and at His word the dead come to life; and that life is invested with mission and crowned in fellowship. So joy becomes the mark of that life. "*I speak these things,*" said Jesus, "*that they may have my joy fulfilled in themselves.*" But how quickly joy turns to sorrow, because truth and love are allowed to conflict with one another. The Church at Ephesus had contended for the truth, but that very strife had ruined its love. "You do not love one another as you did at first," says the Lord amidst the candlesticks. (Rev. 2: 4.) Truth has no saving power except as it becomes the means of sanctity, so that where truth becomes an excuse for strife it becomes a weapon in the hands of the evil one. "*I pray that thou shouldst keep them from the evil one,*" said Jesus. "*Sanctify them in the truth.*"

There is no escape from the world for the disciples of Jesus. Jesus does not allow it. The world will hate them because they are not of the world, but that can be no reason for them to run away. In fact, it is because the world hates them that they know that they are being held true to their essential status as those who do not belong to the world. "*I do not pray,*" said Jesus, "*that thou shouldst take them out of the world. For as thou didst send me into the world, so I have sent them into the world.*" The conflicts of life belong to the very substance of discipleship, and no one must seek to escape from them into the practice of naked religion.

This prayer of Jesus for His disciples must also be our prayer for those whom in His name we seek to win to His discipleship. Too easily we forget that the goal towards which all preaching is set and all witness is given is the creation of missionary communities. The salvation of souls—that is God's business; our business is to participate in His saving ministry and to win participants for it. When Jesus said to the Centurion, "Not even in Israel have I found such faith" (Lk. 7: 9), He was pointing out a truth that every preacher is aware of. There are those, and they are not few, who are not acknowledged believers in Jesus Christ, but whose faith in God and whose obedience to His will put many a Christian to shame. But these too must be won to their missionary calling, for that is their true place in God's economy. Indeed, may it not be that it is because this goal—the creation of missionary communities—has been so largely ignored or forgotten, that our present congregations have also settled down into soliloquy. The Pharisee, in the parable of Jesus, prayed with himself. (Lk. 18: 11.) What else could he do? To use a phrase of Canon Wedel, the religious are quite happy "sitting in heavenly places behind closed doors".[1]

The world is where the disciples of Jesus belong, for it is into the world that He has sent them. There He prays that they must remain: remain to manifest His glory, to extend His name, to contend for His truth, to demonstrate His love, to witness to His unity. And there they can remain and do these things, for He is their sacrifice. "*For their sake,*" says Jesus, "*I consecrate myself, that they also may be consecrated in truth.*" The priest consecrates the victim. Jesus consecrates Himself. Jesus abides in the world dedicated to the task to which He sets His disciples, and they find their dedication made possible by His. The word of God which gave them life and by which they live, that is the truth into which

[1] From article in *The Ecumenical Review*, Vol. IX, no. 3.

they will grow in holiness: and Jesus, through whom that word was spoken, will remain committed to perform it both in the world and in them.

The burden of the missionary calling cannot be discharged simply by one person doing something to another person, or one group doing something to another group. Our witness to the Gospel works by changing both those who witness and those to whom the witness is borne, drawing both together into the unity of a new life. So that where this unity is broken or distorted or does not happen, the success of the missionary calling falls short of its goal. There arises the necessity, then, to cry, "Oh Lord, consecrate us in truth, even as Thou hast consecrated Thyself for our sake."

All consecration is of one piece even as all truth is of one piece, so that the consecration of each disciple is but his share in that one consecration of His Master. That is why Jesus includes in His prayer not only His immediate disciples but also all those who through their word and witness will come to Him. "*I do not pray for these only*," He says, "*but also for those who are to believe in me through their word*." I pray "that they may all be one; even as thou, Father, art in me, and I in thee, that they also may be in us, *so that the world may believe that thou hast sent me*."

Five times in this prayer we find expressed the concern of Jesus that He should be recognized as having been sent by the Father, and that the Father should be recognized as having sent Him. Speaking about His disciples, He says, "*They know in truth that I came from thee; and they have believed that thou didst send me*." Speaking about His disciples' mission, He says, "*As thou didst send me into the world, so I have sent them*." Speaking about the goal of that mission, He says, "I pray that they may all be one *so that the world may believe that thou hast sent me.*" And then praying that His disciples also should be recognized as having been sent by the Father and by Him, He says, "The glory which thou hast given me I have given to them, *that the world may know that thou hast sent me and hast loved them even as thou hast loved me.*" And finally, closing His prayer with a prayer again for His disciples, He says, "O righteous Father, the world has not known thee, but I have known thee; *and these know that thou hast sent me.*"

In this last hour with His disciples before His passion there seems to be just one thing dominating the mind of Jesus, the hope and the prayer that He will be recognized. "Who do you say that I am?" (Mk. 8: 29.) Everything depends on the answer to that question, for this is eternal life "to know thee and to know me whom thou hast sent". "To know"—that is the verb with the most inclusive meaning in Holy Scripture. It means to be committed to, to be possessed by, to search out and understand, to enter in and occupy, to penetrate the mystery of personality and establish fellowship. But at the gateway to this experience stands a sentinel who asks, "Do you know where you are going? Do you know whom you will meet? Are you prepared for the final surrender?"

How much of our preaching skirts round this central issue? Are not we who are preachers the sentinels sent by God into the world and set there to raise these questions with men on God's behalf? And yet, how generally our preaching is concerned with helping men to express their own religiousness rather than with bringing them to an encounter with Jesus Christ! When I was in New Zealand, a few years ago, I went to see the volcanic region around one of its small towns, Rotarua. It was fascinating to watch the boiling mud, and to walk around looking at the various minerals which the erupting volcano had brought out from the bowels of the earth. But the thing that intrigued me most was the sight of men and women living in and around this area who had come to get their dinners cooked over the steam that was arising through small craters scattered all over the place. They brought iron rods which they placed over these craters, and on these rods they set their dinners to be cooked. There was something incongruous about cooking one's dinner on a volcano; but not more incongruous than seeking to harness the power of Jesus Christ in order to run one's own life. The whole aim of religious preaching is to make God relevant to men, to domesticate Him and make Him serve men's needs. The aim of Gospel-preaching, on the other hand, is to make men relevant to God, and to win them for the service of God's purposes. The ultimate concern of the preacher is not men and their needs, not even their religion; his concern is with Jesus Christ who asks that He be known and recognized as having come from the Father.

The witness that produces this result cannot be borne, says Jesus, except as the witnesses abide together. True witness is the witness of the one fellowship. The unity of the fellowship is the result of being loved by the Father even as the Father has loved the Son. This love which binds together into one all those who are loved, and them with Him who loves, is the glory which Jesus says He has given to His disciples. "The glory which thou hast given me," He says, "I have given to them, *that they may be one even as we are one, I in them and thou in me, that they may become perfectly one, so that the world may know that thou hast sent me and hast loved them even as thou hast loved me."*

Speaking of the Servant, Isaiah says, "We esteemed him stricken, smitten by God, and afflicted. But he was wounded for our transgressions . . . with his stripes we are healed." (Is. 53: 4–5.) That was the sign that the Father loved the Son, that He gave the Son to the world. And there can be no other proof that the Father loves us except that He has given us also to the world. The world will recognize and believe that the Father loves us only as it is able to say, "By their stripes I was healed."

The Church is the Servant-community. The world must recognize that this Servant has been appointed by God. It must also be able to recognize that its Servant-hood continues the Servant ministry of the Son whom the Father sent. How is this recognition to come if the love which this Servant-community is seeking to exemplify is not strong enough even to bind this community into one? "The world must see that I have loved them," says Jesus. Does the love of Jesus divide? Truth divides, we say, because we do not believe alike. But why must difference of belief take on institutional expression? "Sanctify them in the truth" was the prayer of Jesus for us. "My truth will set you free" was His promise. So that what we mean by loyalty to the truth cannot be what He meant, since it is producing different results. "In Him," says Archbishop Temple, "we are one; in so far as we are not one we are not yet in Him." [1]

"Father," Jesus prays, *"I desire that they also whom thou hast given me may be with me where I am"*—not only in

[1] *Readings in St. John's Gospel* (Macmillan and Co.), p. 309.

the future but now. "We are," says St. Paul, "hid with Christ in God in the heavenly places." (Cf. Col. 3: 3; Eph. 1: 3.) Did not Jesus himself promise, "A little while, and you will see me no more; again a little while, and you will see me. I go and prepare a place for you, I will come again and will take you to myself, that where I am you may be also. I will not leave you desolate; I will come to you; but if I go, I will send him to you." (John 16: 16; 14: 3, 18; 16: 7.) As we can readily see, here in this promise of Jesus are two guarantees. I will take you, I will come to you. And both these guarantees belong together in one experience. Christian discipleship is exercised both in the fellowship of the Holy Spirit and in the company of the Son—Jesus Christ. Apart from the fellowship of the Holy Spirit there is no deed of discipleship in which we can participate, apart from the company of Jesus Christ there is no one to whom we can be disciples. He works and we work with Him, the Holy Spirit himself preparing the works which we must perform. (Eph. 2: 10.)

There are four ministries of the Church described in the New Testament, and each ministry is shown to be the result of the action of God in Jesus Christ. In Jesus, God has wrought man's salvation. The Church proclaims it; that is its *Kerugma*. In Jesus, God has called men into a new way of life. The Church teaches this way; that is its *Didache*. In Jesus, God has endowed the Church with many gifts. These are the instruments and means of the Church's service to the world. They are its *Charisma*. In Jesus, God has established peace. The Church mediates this peace to men, bringing wholeness and health where there is sin, sickness, division, strife. The *Eirene* of God becomes the task of the Church.

But, says the New Testament, these four ministries of the Church are its ministries only because they are the ministries of the Holy Spirit. It is the Holy Spirit who is the Witness to the *Kerugma*. It is the Holy Spirit who is the Teacher of the *Didache*. It is the Holy Spirit who is the Giver of the *Charisma*. It is the Holy Spirit who is the Mediator of God's *Eirene*.

Already under the themes of *Marturia, Koinonia, Diakonia* and *Leitourgia* we considered the nature of the Church's calling, and we saw how distinctive these were as marks of the life of the Church. The *Marturia* of the Christian was the witness of a victim and not of a spectator. The *Koinonia* of the Christian community was a fellowship that was given and received rather than one which was attained and accomplished. The *Diakonia* of the Church was service rendered to the world not by benefactors but by servants. The *Leitourgia* of the people of God was worship given to God through all that that people did and were. Now, looking at these same activities again in terms of the action of the Holy Spirit, we realize how decisively they determine what the Church is and what it is for. It is for the world, in order that men may be comforted in their distress, in order that they may be led to God's bounty in their need, in order that they may find direction for life amidst their doubts, in order that they may hear the Good News which will end their despair. The prayer of Jesus was that His disciples may be with Him so that they may see His glory. The beginning of the answer to that prayer was when the Holy Spirit came and took possession of them. Then, in all that the Spirit did, they saw the glory of the Son, the glory which the Father gave the Son in His love for Him.

"Communion with God," wrote Professor Hogg after a lifetime experience of missionary service in India,

> does not impel us to make proffer of assistance to the Lord of heaven and earth in some one of His many enterprises that catches our fancy. On the contrary, it evokes in us a spirit compounded of diffidence and eagerness. But once we have heard the word "Go", all diffident hesitancy should disappear. For if I am really and exclusively on the business of the Divine King, all the resources of our Father's empire of Reality must needs be at my call for the legitimate requirements of my errand.

The glory of the Son is, indeed, made manifest by the working of the Spirit and "the faith of Christ's church is challenged to be the medium of God's infinitely resourceful hostility to the calamitous and injurious".[1]

Philip Potter, a young West Indian leader in the Ecumenical Movement, in a letter to one of his friends said this:

> I was struck by the fact that the word *oikoumene* in the Roman Empire stood for the civilized life of the empire—man organized politically, culturally and religiously. The early Church was very aware of this sense of the word when it claimed it for itself. It was as if they were saying that the Gospel and the Church exist to challenge and transform this *oikoumene*, and are in fact a living symbol of what the *oikoumene* might be in the purpose of God.

In other words, the Ecumenical Movement itself is the result of the concern that the Church is obedient to its calling to be in and for the *oikoumene*. To quote Professor

[1] A. G. Hogg, *The Christian Message to the Hindu* (S.C.M. Press), pp. 65, 63.

Hogg again (p. 46), the relation between the gospel and the Church is not only "consequential" but also "integral and constitutive", so that we understand it truly only when we see it as "the nucleus and the nursery of that transformed humanity which shall be fit to be trusted with a transfigured world order". Such is the Divine purpose as the Bible conceives it, and only as we share this perspective shall we also enter into the real inwardness of our Lord's high-priestly prayer.

But in all this prayer of Jesus for His disciples there was one exempted—Judas. Speaking of him, Jesus says, "I am praying for those whom thou hast given me, for they are thine. *I have guarded them, and none of them is lost but the son of perdition, that the scripture might be fulfilled.*" Judas was lost because his very nature was lostness, Jesus had no access to him because Judas was not open to Jesus at all. And yet he too had been given to Jesus by the Father. We may not probe the mystery here concerning Judas, but we must allow it to probe us. For in each one of us lies the possibility of doing what Judas did. And, to the extent that we seek to serve God's will, there also lies the possibility of someone being Judas to us. Can we learn from Jesus to love the betrayer and not forget him also in our prayer? Judas is lost, Jesus tells His Father: but even in his lostness he is within the working of scripture. Nothing happens outside God, not even a man's self-destruction. Indeed, it is this awful truth that we cannot cut ourselves away from God even by desperate sin which is the measure of man's deepest tragedy.

Jesus has prayed for Himself, Jesus has prayed for His disciples, Jesus has prayed for His Church through all time, Jesus has prayed for the world until it is saved: and now, at the end, His prayer closes with a promise,

"I will make Thy name known, *that the love with which thou hast loved me may be in those whom thou dost give me, and I in them.*"

> Give me the love that leads the way,
> The faith that nothing can dismay,
> The hope no disappointments tire,
> The passion that will burn like fire;
> Let me not sink to be a clod:
> Make me Thy fuel, Flame of God.[1]

It was Christmas time when I was preparing these lectures, and just as all preachers do at Christmas I was meditating on the gift of the Christ child. One thing struck me forcibly which I found both in the story of the angel's announcement to Mary as well as his announcement to Zacharias, and that was the fear which the angel's announcement aroused. Mary was afraid when she heard of the gift which God had given her, and so was Zacharias when he heard of the gift that God had given him. Why were they afraid? As I was thinking out the answer to this question, I said to myself, Suppose on Christmas day the angel should appear in my church and tell all of us gathered there, "I have brought each of you a gift, the same gift. When you go home at the close of this Christmas Service, you will find Jesus Christ at home. He will live with you always"—I was sure that at least for myself I should have been sorely afraid.

Every gift, if it is to be enjoyed, involves its own sacrifice. If someone should present my wife with a saree, her first reaction would be, now I need a blouse to match this saree. She would need to spend money on a blouse that she would otherwise have spent on

[1] Amy Carmichael, *Toward Jerusalem* (S.P.C.K. and the Dohnavur Fellowship), p. 94.

something else. If someone should present me with a car, that would put me into great difficulty. There is no room where I live to build a garage, so I shall have to find another house. If someone should present any of you with an elephant it would ruin your life. You could not live in Scotland any more, and that wretched elephant would complicate your life wherever you lived. Of course, my wife can present the saree to someone else, I can give away the motor-car, you can refuse to accept the elephant. But what can we do with Jesus Christ? We can crucify Him. That is what they did in Jerusalem.

This anxiety and fear which Christmas brings is always with us: for it is repeated every time that we receive a gift from God and never more so than when we receive the calling to be preachers. "*I will make Thy name known, that the love with which thou hast loved me may be in them.*" This promise of Jesus is the burden of our calling, and it is a gift which does entail its own sacrifice if we are to make it ours. What that sacrifice is and how it is to be made has been the theme of these lectures. But we cannot end our meditation here, for not even on the success of our sacrifice does anything depend. Everything depends on Him to whom our every obedience belongs and to whom at the last we must commit it.

O'er the harvest reaped or lost
Falls the eve; our tasks are over:
Purpose crowned or purpose crossed,
None may mar and none recover.
Now, O merciful and just,
Trembling lay we down the trust;
Slender fruit of thriftless day,
Father, at Thy feet we lay.

Yea, but Thou, O Judge and Lord,
 Yea, but Thou, O strong and holy,
Take, and in Thy bosom stored,
 By Thy pure hands changing wholly,
  Turn to gold the things of naught,
  Failing deed and failing thought:
  Love, how faint, yet love, we give;
  Thou *within Thee* make it live.[1]

Now unto him that is able to guard you from stumbling, and to set you before the presence of his glory without blemish in exceeding joy, to the only God our Saviour, through Jesus Christ our Lord, be glory, majesty, dominion and power, before all time, and now, and for evermore. Amen. (Jude 24–25, R.V.)

---

[1] John Huntley Skrine (Methodist Hymn Book, 593).

5

The tree was good for food, it was pleasant to the eyes, and it was a tree to be desired to make one wise. So they took the fruit thereof and did eat. And their eyes were opened.

And they heard the voice of the Lord God walking in the garden and they hid themselves from his presence.

And the Lord God called unto Adam, and said unto him, "Where art thou?" And he said, "I heard thy voice in the garden, and I was afraid." Therefore the Lord God sent him forth from the Garden of Eden.

(*See* Gen. 3: 6–9, 23, A.V.)

O merciful God, who hast made all men and hatest nothing that thou hast made, nor wouldest the death of a sinner, but rather that he should be converted and live: have mercy upon us, give us grace to live by thy forgiveness that we may be led into true repentance, and so fetch us home through thy Servant, even Jesus Christ our Lord. Amen.

Adapted from the Third Collect for Good Friday (Book of Common Prayer).

5. God's Servant—Jesus Christ

God, having raised up his servant, sent him to you . . .
to bless you in turning every one of you from your
wickedness. (Acts 3: 26.)

JESUS CHRIST was crucified. But God, the Father,
says St. Peter, raised Him from the dead and sent Him
back to men in order that He may turn them from their
wickedness. The risen and ascended Lord is at work,
and we are called to work with Him.

This work of Christ is the basis of the preacher's
calling. It determines both the nature of his task and
how he will do it. It also determines, and that is its
crucial significance, how the preacher will find his Lord
and experience His fellowship. The key to all Christian
living and obedience is the practice of the presence of
the Master, so that it is well for us to remember where
this presence is promised to us. Jesus promised it in
the worship, the witness, and the service of the Church.
We meet our Lord in the worship of the Eucharist. We
meet Him in the witness of the Word. We meet Him in
the service of the poor. Professor Wolf, in his Christmas
letter for 1957 from the Ecumenical Institute at Bossey,
states this truth very significantly in the following
paragraph:

> Recently we have been thinking [he says] about what
> it means, when Christ says, according to Matt. 25: 34
> and following, that we encounter Him in the "least
> of" His "brethren". We speak of His presence in the
> word and the sacraments. This saying, to which we

ought to give more thought than we do, is disturbing because the "least of these my brethren" are, apparently, the poor, not only in the Church, but everywhere, and perhaps not only those who are poor in material things. It is these that God has loved and for these that Christ died and rose again. So that, when we are now told that it is in these that He is present and awaits us, we can realize the very bodily nature of Christ's solidarity with the world, which began with the Christmas event and continues even now after His ascension. On the other hand, we can realize too the depths of His solidarity with the world; for Christ leads our love towards Himself in the guise of "the least of His brethren".

In this final lecture, it will be our attempt to catch at least a glimpse of the way in which there is thus held together the fact of Christ's presence in the world as its Servant and His presence in the Church as its Lord, so that as we meditate on His work we ourselves may be led to meet Him, and in that meeting find our Master.

The Bible story begins with God's word to Adam, calling to him and saying, "Adam, where art thou?" This same word, with this same search of God for man, continues through the Bible story until, in Jesus Christ, God Himself comes in person to waylay man and turn him from his way.

God is our covenanted God and we, the whole human race, belong to Him. It is with all men that God establishes His covenant when He says, "I will establish my covenant with you; neither shall all flesh be cut off any more." (Gen. 9: 11, R.V.) It was of this covenant that the Biblical writer saw the rainbow to be a symbol, a symbol which appears again at the end of the Bible story where God is revealed as still the God of mercy

with the rainbow arched above His throne. (Rev. 4: 3.)
God will not destroy. The sun of mercy shines amidst
the rain of judgment. God must turn man from his
wickedness so that he may live. The Bible story, from
that first call of God to Adam, is the story of God who
will not let go. He has betrothed himself to man for
better for worse, so that even when men are not true
to this betrothal, He remains true.

Adam, where art thou?

How shall I give thee up, Ephraim?
how shall I deliver thee, Israel?
mine heart is turned within me,
my compassions are kindled together.
I will not execute the fierceness of mine anger,
for I am God and not man.
                    (Hos. 11: 8–9, R.V.)

Hear, O heavens, and give ear, O earth;
I have nourished and brought up children,
and they have rebelled against me.
The ox knoweth his owner,
and the ass his master's crib:
but Israel doth not know,
my people doth not consider.
                    (Is. 1: 2–3, R.V.)

O Jerusalem, Jerusalem,
how often would I have gathered thy children
    together
and ye would not!
                    (Matt. 23: 37, R.V.)

The Lord is not slack concerning his
promise, but is longsuffering, not
wishing that any should perish, but
that all should come to repentance.
                    (2 Pet. 3: 9, R.V.)

God has followed man wherever man has gone and the story of that journey together is the story of man's redemption. Let us follow man as he makes this journey, and God too.

Adam is on his way away from home. The days of innocence are over. Paradise is left behind. And he is beginning his journey to the land of the knowledge of good and evil. Henceforth, he is free from God.

It is in the world, in one's place of employment, in the big cities where men crowd together, in the university, that many a person finds for the first time how important his own thoughts are. He has to live by them. He determines for himself what is good and what is evil, and that which he decides to be he finds that he has to be. There is no more anyone to protect him from himself. In Paradise his freedom was ensured by the limited authority and power which his own decisions had. Parents, teachers and pastors set limits to his freedom. Now there are no limits. He is at the mercy of his own will.

Soon enough he attaches himself to some group or groups. He must escape from the awful power of his aloneness and find protection in the codes of behaviour and patterns of thought of those to whom he makes himself belong. But that is only temporary respite, for God has refused to allow himself to be left behind. The sadness of that voice which said, "Adam, where art thou?" follows him; and from that voice there is no escaping even in the university, even in one's place of employment, even in the big city.

"The Lamb was slain from the foundations of the world." (Rev. 13: 8.) God accompanied man out of Paradise. Having rebelled against being bound by God's command, man has now to live in constant flight from God's pursuit. God is Emmanuel, God with us. (Matt. 1: 23.) He is the inevitable boundary of man's life. We are either prisoners of His word or fugitives from His love.

We know that love. It never departs. It is always there wherever we are and in whatever condition. It is so utterly humble that it is willing to accept any humiliation, so utterly simple that any reason to avoid it is immediately shown to be false. "God, who is rich in mercy, has loved us in Jesus Christ." (Cf. Eph. 2: 4.) There is nothing more that needs to be said.

For Christ Jesus, though He was God, counted it not something to be grasped at to cling to this glory, but emptied himself and became man and was found in the haunts of men. (Cf. Phil. 2: 6–8.) How empty Jesus was, so empty that no one feared to come to Him, and no one had any excuse for keeping away from Him.

> The unclean leper, even from whose shadow men shrank, came to Jesus and Jesus touched him: an action which made Jesus Himself unclean, so that for the stipulated period He could not enter any city.
>
> (Cf. Mk. 1: 40–45.)
>
> Children were brought to Him when He was very tired, but He received them and took them in His arms and blessed them. The Kingdom of God belonged to children and tiredness was no reason to send them away.
>
> (Cf. Mk. 10: 13–16.)

> An adulteress was dragged before Him. He kept His eyes averted from her lest her shame erect a barrier between Him and her: and when she was left alone with Him, He found a way of conveying forgiveness to her.
>
> (Cf. John 8: 3–11.)

> A Pharisee invited Him to dinner, but refused to treat Him as an honoured guest. There was no water for His feet, nor oil for His head, nor was He given the kiss of welcome. But Jesus stayed; and at dinner that night, because of the emptiness of the Christ, God found a way of reaching Simon's soul.
>
> (Cf. Lk. 7: 36–47.)

"He emptied himself." That is the good news of the Christian faith. Only a stable was available, but He came. How else can men meet Him except that He is willing to be among men and with men whatever the situation! But precisely in this emptiness consists also the awkwardness of Jesus. It is because of it that we are unable to keep Him away from our lives. We satisfy ourselves by offering Him a stable, and hope that He will not come to be a permanent guest, but He comes. In our work, in our thoughts, in our plans, often even in our prayers, there is only a stable for Him, and yet He is there.

The Church in the world, the Christian group in the business office, the fellowship of Christians in the university: these are set as common stables where the Christ will come: and, because the Christ comes, these become wherever they are an echo to men of those words spoken to Adam, "Adam, where art thou?" The Lamb was slain from the foundations of the world. God accompanied man out of Paradise. So that each man, whoever he is and wherever he is, must come to terms with God.

What shall men do? Each man takes his own road, but all men find that whatever road they take, it leads back to Him, and this time to Gethsemane. It is to Gethsemane that the road from Bethlehem leads, the road by which Jesus comes; it is also to Gethsemane that the road from Paradise leads, the road by which Judas arrives. Here in Gethsemane, God and man meet again.

The intervening years have been filled with joy and sorrow, hopes aroused and hopes shattered, attempts to come to terms with Christ and attempts to force Him to come to terms with oneself, thoughts of discipleship and thoughts of disloyalty. But the final issue still remains to be settled, and it lies in that garden to which Jesus has come and where He has decided that Judas shall meet Him.

"Adam, where art thou?"—that is how the story began: "Friend, why are you here?"—that is how the story comes to its crisis.

> Jesus came to the disciples and said to them, "Are you still sleeping? Behold the hour is at hand and my betrayer is near."
>
> Then came Judas, and with him a great crowd with swords and clubs, and he came up to Jesus and kissed Him. Jesus said to him, "Friend, why are you here?"
> (Cf. Matt. 26: 45–50.)

Judas had committed himself to a cause which was the cause of his people. God would restore the Kingdom to

Israel, and God's Messiah would come. So that, in accepting to follow Jesus, Judas accepted Him as the answer to all his plans and all his hopes. Here was a discipleship which commanded all that he had to give. But Jesus had broken loose from the plans that Judas had made for Him, and the freedom which Judas had contrived which was built on imprisoning God, now lay shattered because Jesus had His own way which He would take.

Jesus comes even if it be a stable we have to offer, but we cannot make Him at home there. It is our stable until He comes, but once He comes it is His territory, the spearhead of His thrust into the whole area of our lives. No wonder that we seek the only way out which is possible, which is to betray Him.

Have you been to Gethsemane? Do you know what it means to betray the Son of Man as your last desperate attempt to make Him serve your ends? Do your lips tremble at the remembrance of that kiss which you gave Him when you sought to deliver Him over to His enemies in order that you may keep Him for yourself? Or is it your situation that you have not still arrived at Gethsemane, that you still find it possible to support the company of Jesus without feeling any radical opposition to Him and without encountering any radical opposition between His plans and your own?

Only those who have stood face to face with Jesus at Gethsemane know the devastating power of the words with which He greeted them: "Friend, why are you here?"—and the overwhelming humility with which He allowed them to take Him captive. "He emptied himself, and being found in human form he humbled himself and became obedient unto death." How often we have seen this event take place in the lives of many whom we know! God at man's mercy because God will not leave man alone even on his journey away from Paradise; and man therefore seeking ways of rejecting God, of ejecting Him!

It is in Gethsemane that we discover that we are rebels; and that discovery we must make. Some day each one of us must see, if we have not already so seen, how brittle is our moral nature, how deceitful are our intellectual processes, and how possessive is even the very dedication by which we live. And this vision will not come until we see ourselves as Judas saw himself, when, standing afar off, he watched Him die whom he had betrayed.

Jesus Christ emptied Himself, He became ours. He humbled Himself, He put Himself at our mercy. He was obedient unto death, He accepted the fate we had decreed for Him. Is it any wonder that He calls Himself our servant and demands that we accept His service if we wish to have anything to do with Him at all? It is easy to call Him Lord; it is difficult to accept Him as servant. That night when He washed the feet of the disciples, Simon Peter would not allow Him to wash his feet. Jesus said to him, "Simon, if I do not wash you, you have no part in me." (John 13: 8.) You must accept the service I have come to bring. For the Son of Man came not to be ministered unto but to minister and to give his life a ransom for many. (Mk. 10: 45.) The Hindu finds it easy to speak of Jesus as God incarnate, but he will not accept Him as Saviour. The Buddhist is willing to speak of the Lord Jesus, but he will not accept His grace. The Muslim is willing to speak of Isa Nabi, but he will not accept His forgiveness.

Authority can take many forms. A mother's authority over her child is the authority of one who serves. So is the authority of Jesus. It took the form of a servant.

We need to be broken by the humility of Jesus before we can realize who He is and what it is that He wants from us. Is Jesus your servant? Has He done for you what you could not do for yourself? Is He doing for you what you cannot do for yourself? To ask the age-old question: "Are you washed in the blood of the Lamb?"

> I looked, and behold a great multitude, from every nation, from all tribes and peoples and tongues, clothed in white robes with palm branches in their hands, and crying out with a loud voice, "Salvation belongs to our God and to the Lamb!"

> Who are these, clothed in white robes? These are they who have washed their robes and made them white in the blood of the Lamb. Therefore are they before the throne of God, and serve Him day and night.
>
> (Rev. 7: 9–15.)

Thus the journey of man proceeds: from Paradise through the dusty roads of Galilee to Gethsemane, and from Gethsemane along the *via dolorosa* to Calvary, and from Calvary—where? Judas went and bought the potter's field and hanged himself. (Acts 1: 18a; Matt. 27: 5b.) He could bear no longer the love of Jesus Christ. But, oh how wasteful that was, wasteful of his life, wasteful of his repentance, wasteful of God's forgiving grace! Judas could not forget himself even in his repentance. Even in his repentance, he had to be master of his own life.

We don't truly repent until we have received that repentance itself as a gift from Him (2 Tim. 2: 25b), as part of His service to us, and so find ourselves delivered finally from being at the mercy of our own will. And then? And then, along the paths of our obedience as well as our disobedience, we meet Him, the Lord of our lives as He is the Lord of life, whose will for us has become again the acknowledged boundary of our existence, and we find Paradise again in the mastery of His fellowship. Saul was on his way to Damascus, Jesus met him along the way. (Acts 9: 1–6.) So to us too it will happen that He will meet us on every Damascus road, waylaying us along life's journey when we take the wrong turning, even sending us blindness with respect to those things which He will not have us undertake, and asking us to go to the house which He has prepared for us where it shall be told us what we must do.

Within God's house, the fellowship of the Church— there our journey ends: and begins.

> Blessed be the God and Father of our Lord Jesus Christ, who through Jesus Christ destined us in love to be His sons according to the purpose of His will; and sealed us with the Holy Spirit the guarantee of our inheritance; to the praise of His glorious grace which He freely bestowed on us in the Beloved. Amen.
>
> (Eph. 1: 3–14.)

The grace of the Lord Jesus Christ, and the love of God, and the communion of the Holy Ghost, be with you all. Amen. (2 Cor. 13: 14, R.V.)

Postscript

O God of infinite mercy, who hast compassion on all men, hear the prayers of thy servants, who are unworthy to ask any petition for themselves, yet are in duty bound to pray for others: let thy mercy descend upon the Church; that her sacrifice of prayer and thanksgiving may ever ascend to thy throne.

Forgive our enemies and help us to forgive. Comfort the afflicted; speak peace to troubled consciences; strengthen the weak; confirm the strong; instruct the ignorant; deliver the oppressed; relieve the needy; and bring us all by the waters of comfort and in the ways of righteousness to thy eternal Kingdom; through Jesus Christ our Lord. Amen.

After Jeremy Taylor.

Summons at Midnight[1]

Which of you who has a friend will go to him at midnight and say to him, "Friend, lend me three loaves; for a friend of mine has arrived on a journey, and I have nothing to set before him"?

(Lk. 11: 5–6.)

IT is midnight in the parable. It is also midnight in the world to-day. The night is so deep that everything has become just an object to be avoided, an obstacle in the dark against which men must take care not to bump. Certainly, there are those who are blaring out guidance: but the guidance offered is so confusing that wisdom seems to lie in not accepting any of it. The hour of midnight is the hour when all cows are black, and he is a good prophet who simply tells men what not to do.

Besides, at midnight, every colour loses its distinctiveness and becomes merely a dirty shade of grey. There is to-day so much disappointment and disillusion, so much frustration and bewilderment, that cynicism and despair have taken possession of many men's souls. Nothing seems to matter. They do not in the dark. Honesty, chastity, sobriety, courtesy—these deal with distinctions in human behaviour which tend to become irrelevant when it is a long midnight: and men at midnight listen easily only to those who speak about the tragedy of life.

[1] Address delivered at the Evanston Assembly of the World Council of Churches, 1954.

Also, at midnight, nobody expects anything to happen. It is the hour when no-happening is good news. How anxiously, in whatever part of the world we live, we read our newspapers; and, as we put them down, we heave a sigh of relief. Nothing has happened. Everywhere the unresolved problems continue to stand on end and nowhere have they toppled over into violent activity or event. So midnight drags on with our ears strained in the hope that they will hear no sound.

But, as in the parable, so in our day, the tense silence of midnight is disturbed by the sound of a knock. It is the door of the Church on which somebody is knocking. That is still the one familiar landmark to which the traveller by midnight comes. How bitterly men and women speak about their disappointment with the Church! They may be right or wrong: but at least in this their attitude is significant that they feel that the Church should not have disappointed them. It is the one house which stands where it has always stood, the house to which the man travelling at midnight either comes or refuses to come. Many decide not to come; some, however, come and knock; and those who decide not to come are still preoccupied with the Church which they have rejected.

God has set the Church as a city is set upon a hill. He has made it an object of decision. If men are not so foolish as to light a lamp and put it under a bushel, God is not less wise. He has set His Church as a lamp is set upon a stand.

But, is it only individuals who knock at the door of the Church? What, for instance, is the truth about this Assembly of the World Council of Churches? Whose knocking has compelled the Churches to gather here? Too exclusively and too easily we conceive the Christian task as that of seeking and finding the lost, so that we are constantly preoccupied about going out to do it. We do not sufficiently realize that the evangelistic situation is again and again that of being surrounded and sought after and questioned. There are those who are knocking at the door of the Church; and they are not merely the hungry, the homeless, the refugee, the displaced person, the outcast; there are at the Church's door, also, every type of community—nations, races, classes, political groupings—knocking for different reasons. Some are asking for bread, others simply ask what kind of people live in this house in which a light shines at midnight, and still others come just to shake their fists in the faces of those who keep a light burning but have no bread.

For it is true that so often there is no bread in the house. The Church is expecting no callers and has laid in no supplies. With what bread it had it has just managed to feed its own children. It has sufficient obedience not to put out the light in the window, but it does not have sufficient expectancy to believe that anybody will come.

Unfortunately, however, there is also the other fact that so many members of the Church get worried when the Church tries to prepare to welcome all callers. A year ago (1953) the Ceylon government lifted its subsidy on rice, and the political parties of the left declared a day's *hartal* in protest, a day's general stoppage of work. Some hooliganism broke out and the government used force to quell the disturbances. It was the kind of situation in which most people were concerned with policy and expediency, and where the common mass of people felt helpless to think or speak in terms of what was right or wrong. Their silence and helplessness knocked at the door of the Church. The Methodist Church in Ceylon heard the knock, woke up, and spoke to the situation in the name of Jesus Christ. Immediately the question was raised, "Should not the Church have kept quiet? After all, it is midnight, and nothing that the Church says or does will make any difference!"

It is true, isn't it, that there are those who bear the name of Jesus Christ who want the Church not to answer any call but the call of private personal need or the call for salvation after death? Here at this Assembly, the Churches have come together to speak on the questions put to the Church on international affairs, on racial and ethnic tensions, on social and economic problems, on the issues of Church unity and disunity— and surely the Churches are right in this undertaking. "God so loved the world that He gave His Son." So that the task of the Church is to proclaim God's Son as the hope of the world. This means that Jesus is the hope of men in all the complexities of their relationships to one another, and that Jesus is the hope also of the Church precisely when the Church is engaged in setting forth Jesus as the hope of the world.

Evangelism means that the Christian community, by all that it does and says and is, brings to bear the truths of the Gospel on the torments of the world. It means that thus the pressure of the Gospel upon the world is maintained, so that the solution to every human problem—whether it be the problem of war-torn Korea or the problem of a widowed mother who does not have the wherewithal to feed her children—may be worked out under that pressure by those whose responsibility it is to work them out. It is a question wrongly put when it is asked, "What is the Christian solution which the

Church can offer to this or that problem?" for the task of the Church is not to offer Christian solutions to specific problems but to incarnate the Word in every human situation. The result of such witness may be that the Word is crucified, but Jesus must go to Jerusalem and suffer many things and be killed and on the third day be raised. (Mk. 10: 33, 34.) Pilate had power to send Jesus to his death: but Pilate had no power to prevent the resurrection. The hope of the world is Jesus whom the world has the power to crucify: and it is this hope in this manner which the Church is constrained to proclaim. The Church lives and works by the promise of Jesus that to it is given to share in the cup that He drank and in the baptism with which He was baptized. (Mk. 10: 39.)

The Church's attempt to escape from its responsibility to the world is again and again the result of seeking to dodge this issue of the cross, and when that happens the Church ceases to understand the true dimension of the hope that is in Christ. Only a Church that is truly evangelistic knows or can speak about the Christian hope, nor is it possible to believe in the Gospel except as one shares in its operation in the world.

When the Church ceases to be concerned with the world, then it ceases to hear God speak to it; for God's conversation with the Church is a conversation about the world, and the Church must be willing to converse about the world if it is to converse with God. It is the world which is the direct object of God's action. He made it. He loved it. He saved it. He will judge it through Jesus Christ. Indeed, a Church that is disobedient to its commission to go to the world becomes a menace to the world itself. Disobedient Jonah was the cause of the storm that overtook that ship on its normal trading voyage, and those sailors had no other alternative but to throw him into the sea. (Jonah 1 : 12.) Even this is part of God's providence; when the world casts the Church overboard and leaves it at God's mercy.

The Church may not escape its commission to be the friend. "A friend of mine has arrived on a journey." So speaks the man in the parable, and, in so speaking, defines the attitude of true evangelism.

Whoever comes and whenever he comes, comes as a friend : and he comes because we have turned ourselves into friends. Have we not found that when we Christians begin really to desire to share our friendship with Jesus Christ with others, when we give ourselves to expectant prayer asking God to help us to find new friends for Jesus, when we take seriously the need of keeping watch over ourselves lest they who come to us find no evidence of our friendship either with Jesus Christ or with them—that then the experience of evangelism becomes not so much the experience of going out to find as that of being ready to welcome those who come ?

Jesus said, "Other sheep I have which are not of this fold; them also I must bring", and He is out over mountain and plain and across the seas looking for these sheep (John 10: 16); and wherever there is an open Christian door He brings the sheep there for them to find pasture. "A friend has come"—those are the words of the parable; but the friend, who came, came because Jesus knew that a friend was waiting, and He brought the weary traveller to that friendly door. In reading the parable of the Good Samaritan (Lk. 10: 30–35) have you not wondered what it must have meant to the innkeeper to have a wounded man thrust on his care so suddenly? But the innkeeper was a friend, and the Samaritan must have known his ready friendship in order to bring to him with such confidence and with so little warning the man that had fallen among thieves. It is Jesus who is the evangelist: we but keep the door of the fold, we but keep the inn on the road; and where there is expectant love there are always callers, those whom Jesus brings. And how many are the ways, unexpected ways, in which He brings them!

I learned that someone who was a college-mate with me had drifted away from the Christian faith. He had had a very difficult experience in his home which was the cause of it, and I was anxious to bring to him again a witness to the joy of the Gospel. I met him many times, but the occasions were not casual or convenient enough for a heart-to-heart conversation. I kept on praying about it until, after two years, it happened one day that he and I found ourselves sitting next to each other in a crowded railway compartment bound on a long journey. The opportunity had come. The friend had arrived brought there by Jesus.

The Ashram in Jaffna, the town in Ceylon from which I come, opened last year an evangelistic mission among the Veddahs, the aboriginal tribe of Ceylon. There it is a contest between the power of the Gospel in the whole life of man and primitive belief in the power of demons. There was in the place a Hindu devotee who was the centre of no-response to the Christian work that was being done. How were his co-operation and sympathy to be won? One day his son, going out into the forest to gather honey, got stung by forest wasps. It was known to be fatal to be stung like that. The boy, running away in headlong flight, came to the Ashram settlement. A crowd gathered. The mother of the boy was sent for. But there was nothing anybody could do. There were no medicines, no doctors, in a place so far away from anywhere. The body of the boy began to swell. The Christian evangelist in charge of the place had a cup of hot coffee made, gave it to the boy, knelt down and began to pray. As the prayer went on, the boy quietened down; soon he was breathing without panting, and in two hours' time he went home with his mother perfectly whole. The next morning the father arrived, full of apologies and bursting with thanks. A friend had been won to the cause of Christ. Christ had brought him to the door of a friend.

There are many causes for the lack of results in evangelistic work, but the primary cause always is failure in expectant love. Often, we do not care about people as people sufficiently enough. We are concerned about evangelism, but this concern is largely the consequence of a desire to fulfil our evangelistic duty as Christians. But evangelism, in order to be true evangelism, must cease to be a duty. It must become an inevitability. The shepherd looking for his lost sheep is not fulfilling a duty. A mother praying for her erring child is not meeting an obligation. A church declaring God's judgments to the people is not just obeying a call. A friend sharing his friendship with Jesus is not simply discharging a responsibility. "The love of Christ controls us," says St. Paul, "and if I do not preach the Gospel I shall burst." (Cf. 2 Cor. 5: 14; 1 Cor. 9: 16.) Jeremiah's eyes were full of tears as he declared God's judgments to his people. He loved them.

It is so easy to engage oneself in what are known as

evangelistic activities, to have even a true theology of evangelism, and yet be and remain the kind of person into whose hands the Great Shepherd cannot entrust His sheep. Let me put the question in this way. Can you mention the names of the people—two or three perhaps—who are to you a cause of real sorrow because they are not Christians? They are good people, they are your friends, but always when you think of them there is a pain in your soul because they do not serve Jesus Christ. Are there such people in your life? If not, you are not an evangelist however much may be the evangelistic work which you do.

This emphasis on the impulse of evangelism is also of significance where the so-called foreign missionary enterprise is concerned. There is a world of difference between the missionary who comes to proclaim the truth of the Gospel and the missionary who comes to care for a people with the care of Jesus Christ.

And the heart of the experience for every evangelist lies also just here, that it is when we are really concerned with people as people that we discover our own poverty too. We have speeches, arguments, techniques; schools, hospitals, orphanages; books, pamphlets, posters; but of love and real care we do not have what is necessary to meet the need. As in the parable, so we are driven to say, "A friend has arrived and I have nothing to set before him." We cannot feed them on scraps, we love too truly to do that.

But there is another Friend to whom we may go, one who has promised to provide us with bread whenever we ask. "Ask," He said, "and it will be given you; seek, and you will find; knock, and it will be opened to you. For if you who are evil know how to give good gifts to your children, how much more will the heavenly

Father give the Holy Spirit to those who ask Him?"
(Lk. 11: 9, 13.)

The answer to the prayer for the Holy Spirit is
always, "Yes." There is always bread with Him who
is the bread of life. And He gives it to those who ask.
Our problem is that we forget that we cannot feed our
friends who come to us out of our own sufficiency, or
that we do not know the way to our other Friend's
home sufficiently well in order to run to Him in a
hurry. The evangelist must be a man of prayer or he
will never find the bread with which to feed the hungry.

But it is precisely here that we must reckon with
another truth, a truth which any evangelist, who has
gone to Jesus asking for bread, knows: for, again and
again, the answer of Jesus to the request for bread is
this, "Friend, a large supper is ready; therefore go and
bring your friend and not only him, but bring many
others also."

> For the kingdom of heaven may be compared to a
> king who gave a marriage feast for his son. And he
> said to his servants, "The wedding is ready. Go there-
> fore to the thoroughfares and invite to the marriage
> feast as many as you find." And those servants went
> out into the streets and gathered all whom they found,
> both bad and good; so the wedding hall was filled
> with guests. (Matt. 22: 1, 8–10.)

Bread, for those whom Jesus will bring to our door; and
bread for those whom Jesus bids us go and find and
bring to His door: both are indivisible parts of the one
task. We have no bread, but He gives the Holy Spirit
to them that ask Him. A supper is going to waste, a
supper which God gave His Son to die on the cross to
prepare: therefore, "go out to the highways and hedges
and compel people to come in".

Some who are hungry will come asking for bread, but many who are equally hungry must have the bread taken to them. "Do you believe in Jesus?" we ask someone whom we would win for the Kingdom: we get no answer, for the question in his heart is "Does Jesus believe in me?" The evangelist must know how to say and say convincingly, "Yes, my friend, Jesus does believe in you and He is waiting for you. Come."

But just what does it mean that the Master says to us, "Go, and compel people to come in"? What does it mean that we are ordered to succeed? Surely we are here face to face with the basic contradiction in which the evangelist is involved, the contradiction between the command to succeed in his mission to those to whom he is sent and the need to be faithful to the message with which he is entrusted. The truth is that many who are invited will not come, and that the Master will not send His invitation back to them in a more acceptable form. Our faithfulness to Jesus Christ does set limits on our search for successful evangelistic methods, but even so does the love of God for every man drive us to seek for methods which will be more successful.

Jesus was led up by the Spirit into the wilderness to be tempted by the devil (Matt. 4: 1) and the temptations arose because He must succeed in that which He came to do and because He must also be faithful to His Father who sent Him. Our serious temptations, too, lie just where we are led by the Spirit.

By way of illustration, let us look at a pervasive feature of the human situation to-day, a situation which seems to be a characteristic of this midnight hour at which we live. For countless men and women the natural context of their lives has been destroyed. Family and neighbourhood no longer determine how life is lived. Rather, the determining factors are the companions with whom they work, the clubs of which they are members, the gangs to which they belong. When the evangelist succeeds with people like this, there arise congregations of Christians whose form of existence calls into question the normal structure of the parish. Do we see where the path of obedience lies in this situation? We must be faithful, we must also succeed. What shall we do? Our present problem, and it is an urgent one, is that in situation after situation of this kind, where evangelistic experiment has pointed to uncharted ways or called into question accepted structures, the Churches are in large measure refusing to be led by the Spirit into the wilderness there to be tempted by the devil. They seem to prefer to go to the cross some other way.

Midnight is a difficult hour in which to be faithful or successful: but we shall find grace as we seek to minister to the real need of him who comes to us in the midnight. For the traveller by midnight who is asking for bread is really asking for the dawn; and bread is only until it dawns. What is his need? Let me answer with a story. I was returning home from the office one day, and I saw my elder son, then four years of age, sitting out on the doorstep. He followed me as I entered the house, and trailed behind me as I went in and was speaking to my wife. He stood there for a few minutes, then suddenly said to his mother, "Mamma, why don't you tell papa what I did?" I asked my wife, "Why, what has he done?" She smiled and said, "He broke the jam-pot to-day." He had been sitting out on the doorstep waiting for his father because the jam-pot was on his conscience. There is only one person who can set us free from our past and that is He who is our judge. Once He comes, and once He knows, we are free. Will He come?

> Watchman, what of the night?
>
> The morning comes.
>
> Amen, Lord Jesus, Come.
> (Is. 21: 11, 12; Rev. 22: 20.)

The God of all grace, who called you unto his eternal glory in Christ, after that ye have suffered a little while, shall himself perfect, stablish, strengthen you. To him be the dominion for ever and ever. Amen.

(1 Pet. 5: 10–11, R.V.)

Index

141